Breathing In

Breathing Out

Breathing In, Breathing Out

Keeping a Writer's Notebook

Ralph Fletcher

HEINEMANN
Portsmouth, NH

Heinemann
A division of Reed Elsevier Inc.
361 Hanover Street
Portsmouth, NH 03801-3912

Offices and agents throughout the world

Acknowledgments for borrowed material can be found on page 99.

Library of Congress Cataloging-in-Publication Data

Fletcher, Ralph J.
    Breathing in, breathing out : keeping a writer's notebook / Ralph Fletcher.
        p.   cm.
    Includes bibliographical references.
    ISBN 0-435-07227-7
    1. English language—Rhetoric.   2. Notebooks.   I. Title.
PE1408.F49   1996
808'.02—dc20   96-9786
                                                           CIP

Editor: Carolyn Coman
Copy editor: Alan Huisman
Production: Vicki Kasabian
Book design: Mary C. Cronin
Cover design: Jenny Jensen Greenleaf
Cover photo: Jay Paul
Manufacturing: Louise Richardson

Printed in the United States of America on acid-free paper

05 04 03   DA   13 12 11

to Don Murray
whose encouragement
and wise friendship
have made a difference

Contents

I know journal writing works for me in the sense that on a daily basis I am taking what happens in my head, running it down through my heart, then up through my shoulder, down my arm, and into my fingers that hold my pen. I like the physicality of writing by hand, the act of translating what I'm feeling and thinking into words on a page. Writing daily, or almost daily, no matter what comes out, makes me feel whole, purposeful, balanced, scrubbed clean. There is so much about the process of writing that is mysterious to me, but this is one thing I've found to be true: Writing begets writing.

Dorianne Laux

Acknowledgments

Several people were helpful in making this book snap into focus:

Toby Gordon. Toby gave me important encouragement early in this project.

Mike McCormick. During a trip to Eagle River, Alaska, Mike and I had many conversations about writer's notebooks. Mike also helped me locate important material by and about William Stafford.

Carolyn Coman. It's amazing that my Heinemann editor for this book should also be one of my favorite writers. I admire both of Carolyn's books, *Tell Me Everything* and *What Jamie Saw*, a Newbery Honor Book. She turned out to be a terrific editor, warm and literate, who entered into the spirit of this book. Carolyn both supported and stretched me; this is a far better book because of her.

JoAnn Portalupi. In addition to all her other attributes, my wife is a skilled editor, both generous and demanding. Her close readings of my drafts were enormously helpful in shaping the final text.

Don Murray. I have no doubt that Don could have written (and may still write) his own book about writer's notebooks. But in all my talks with him he never made me feel as if I were intruding on his territory. He generously opened up his personal library to me, pointed me toward many invaluable sources, and read this book in manuscript. More than anything, Don showed genuine interest in this project. His wisdom breathes through so much of my work, written and unwritten. I feel lucky to call him friend.

First Thoughts

When my children were born the act of following a poem through from start to finish in one place became a thing of the past. Learning to use the notebook as a safe deposit box—a place to put half an image or a fraction of a line for safekeeping—was vital and helpful.

Eavan Boland

Keeping a notebook is the single best way I know to survive as a writer. It encourages you to pay attention to your world, inside and out. It serves as a container to keep together all the seeds you gather until you're ready to plant them. It gives you a quiet place to catch your breath and begin to write.

In his book *Freedom to Learn* Carl Rogers suggests the need for a college course on the caring and feeding of infant ideas: "Creative thoughts and actions are just like infants: unprepossessing, weak, easily knocked down. A new idea is always very inadequate compared to an established one."

Most of my ideas for poems, stories, novels, or essays sound pretty iffy (pretty awful) at their earliest stage; I suspect this is true for most writers. But those early rumblings, farfetched visions, the faint scratchings of the imagination, are crucial for a writer who hopes to create something original. How do you keep those ideas alive until you're ready to use them?

A notebook can work as a safe haven for your infant ideas in exactly the way Rogers suggests. It gives you a place to incubate very new ideas before they are strong and mature enough to face the harsh light of rational judgment, let alone public scrutiny. And it's an ideal place for the very brief writing stretches most of us have to squeeze into our frenetic lives.

Many writers use some form of notebook and consider it an essential part of their creative process. The nomenclature, however, can get confusing. Some writers talk interchangeably about a *journal, diary, sketchbook, notebook,* or *daybook*; others make subtle distinctions between these terms. I met one schoolgirl who spoke enthusiastically about her *lifebook*. For simplicity and consistency I have opted for the generic term *writer's notebook*.

That's what this book is about: *What is the writer's notebook? How do writers use it? What makes it tick?* I draw from my own notebook entries as well as the notebook entries of other writers. In this way I have tried to show a range of possibilities. When one of my entries rubs shoulders with an entry by an F. Scott Fitzgerald or other literary luminary, I hope you will forgive my temerity. I include selections from my notebook not as examples of immortal writing but in the spirit of revealing the "displayed self" of the writer whose innermost workings I know best.

I consider metaphors crucial tools to help readers get a feel for any subject, particularly one as amorphous as the writer's notebook. This book puts forth a profusion of metaphors. Grab the most helpful ones and ignore the rest.

The book's title illuminates two basic aspects of the writer's notebook. *Breathing In* refers to the way the notebook serves as a container for selected insights, lines, images, ideas, dreams, and fragments of talk gathered from the world around you. In this way it gets you into the habit of paying closer attention to your world. *Breathing Out* suggests that the notebook is a fine place from which to take what you have collected and use it to spark your own original writing.

Although the chapters at the beginning of the book tend to focus on breathing in (collecting) and the latter chapters on breathing out (generating), many chapters explore both aspects of the notebook. A breath, after all, has two parts; you can't breathe in without breathing out. It's my hope that this book helps you find a natural rhythm for using a notebook in your writing life.

I very nearly titled this book *First Person*, borrowed from the title of a commencement address Anna Quinlan gave at Wellesley College. I liked that. First person suggests the tone I want for this book: the conversational "I" of a writer, up close and intimate. And first person also offers a revealing glimpse into the nature of the writer's notebook itself. The notebook is a no-strings-attached gift to the I/eye.

"Our notebooks give us away," Joan Didion writes in *Slouching Towards Bethlehem*, "for however dutifully we record what we see around us, the common denominator of all we see is always, transparently, shamelessly, the implacable 'I.' "

Your notebook is a room of your own. It encourages you to inhabit that first person pronoun fully and without apology. It provides a safe place for you to ask: *What do I notice? What do I care about? What moves the deepest part of me? What do I want to remember for the rest of my life? What do I want to write about? How might I begin?*

First person also touches on the question of the audience. As a young writer I dreamed of seeing my name on the cover of a book. Any book. Rereading my notebooks, I now see that the first, most important audience for my writing has always been me. During the lean years before I had published anything, my notebook gave me a writing arena. A safe, nonthreatening place where I never got graded, laughed at, or rejected. It gave me a place to develop the habits of a writer, to take my work seriously. Writing in my notebook, I discovered that I could take real pleasure in what I put down on paper, could sustain my spirits on the enjoyment derived from working my craft.

This book is for new writers, but it is also for those of us who used to write but stopped writing. I have talked with many people who loved to write at one time in their lives but now find themselves in a world where they write only memos, briefs, or advertisements. Somewhere along the way they lost their love of writing.

Have you forgotten when writing was fun? When your writing had zest and nerve? When the words you wrote cut so close to your heart it pounded as your hands formed the letters?

First person: writing for yourself, for the pleasure you take in the craft. This reminds me of a poem by David Fisher about a circus bear:

The Bear
Thrown from the boxcar of the train, the bear
rolls over and over. He sits up
rubbing his nose. This must be
some mistake,
     there is no audience here.
He shambles off through the woods.

    *   *   *

The forest is veined with trails,
he does not know which to follow.
The wind is rising, maple leaves turn up
their silver undersides in agony, there is a
smell in the air, and the lightning strikes.
He climbs a tree to escape. The rain
pours down, the bear is blue as a gall.

    *   *   *

There is not much to eat
in the forest, only berries,
and some small delicious animals
that live in a mound and bite your nose.

    *   *   *

The bear moves sideways through a broom-straw field.
He sees the hunters from the corner of his eye
and is sure they have come to take him back.
To welcome them, (though there is no calliope)
he does his somersaults, and juggles

a fallen log, and something
                tears through his shoulder,
he shambles away in the forest and cries.
Do they not know who he is?
          *   *   *
After a while, he learns to fish, to find
the deep pool and wait for the silver trout.
He learns to keep his paw up for spiderwebs.
There is only one large animal, with trees
on its head, that he cannot scare.
            *   *   *
At last he is content to be
alone in the forest,
though sometimes he finds a clearing
and solemnly does his tricks,
though no one sees.

A notebook can be a clearing in the forest of your life, a place where you can be alone and content as you play with outrage and wonder, details and gossip, language and dreams, plots and subplots, perceptions and small epiphanies. I hope this book will encourage you to start a notebook and use it in ways that nourish your writing life. I hope it helps reawaken the writer in you. You won't find any clever formulas or neat recipes in these pages. But if you have ever been intrigued by the idea of keeping a writer's notebook, this book will give you a place to start.

1

A Place to Write

I'm sure a beautiful empty notebook was the reason I wrote my first book. It was begging for filling.

Jacqueline Jackson

At home I write in an office separated from the rest of the house by a glass door two panes thick. This situates me only a few feet from the loud spiritual center of our house—the breakfast bar. Fortunately, on most writing days I am home alone. Except for the telephone the house stays quiet; usually, I can work.

In *The Writing Life* Annie Dillard says: "Appealing workplaces are to be avoided. One wants a room with no view so memory can dance with imagination in the dark."

Great thought—but I hope she's wrong. My office has eleven long windows that offer gorgeous views on three sides. When I reach for my coffee mug I get glimpses of grass and sun-dappled woods that offer uncountable shades of green or brown or white at every turn of the season. When the snowflakes fall or autumn leaves come swirling down I sometimes get the sensation of weightlessness, my desk and I free-falling through space.

The view is terrific but I don't spend much time looking out. Or rather, when I'm looking out I'm actually looking in—ruminating on whatever I'm writing about. I think of that physical place as part of a series of concentric circles: earth, home, office, desk, screen, passage, word, and the urge behind the word.

As much as I have always admired the Spartan ideal of the empty desk, I can never quite pull it off. A share of the family's flotsam and jetsam always finds its way onto mine; I push back the worst of it before I get started. But there are some things I don't want to clear off. I find it soothing to have certain objects close by while I write:

- Photograph of me at five years old with four younger siblings.
- Trilobite fossils, each a couple hundred million years old.
- Arrowheads crafted by the Native Americans who once walked this land. Legend has it that way back my ancestors, the Fletchers from England, were skilled arrow makers. Today the feathered part of the arrow is known as the *fletching*.
- Rocks. I keep some because they are embedded with crystals, others because of their heft, smoothness, the way they feel. These rocks have a way of finding their way into my hands whenever my words begin to feel false and empty.
- Snakeskin. I have a snakeskin from a garter snake pinned to the wooden frame of the window above me. I love its translucency and lightness; the slightest breeze will make it sway this way or that. The snake decided he no longer needed it, but I do. In its way it tells me: *Risk everything. Outgrow yourself.*
- Owl pellet. A teacher read my poem "Owl Pellets" (in *I Am Wings*) and sent this one to me. It is brown, roughly the size and color of a Brazil nut, and ugly as a turd. I figure I'll hang onto it until it starts to smell. I can't bring myself to get rid of it. The owl pellet reminds me of all the indigestible things, the bones of experience, lurking in my head. It's up to me to dig them out. Reconstruct them.
- Notebook. It sits on the far left corner of my desk. Mine is black and brown, each page lined and numbered. What the notebook lacks in physical beauty it makes up for in sturdiness; it was meant to be a business ledger, built to last.

Novelist Po Bronson likes to use "stealth notebooks" two and a half inches by five inches. These have the advantage of being supremely portable—tuck them into any pocket and off you go.

8

There is nothing sleek or stealthy about my notebook. It's a big clunky one, much too big to tuck into my back pocket for a hike or a weekend drive. I love the idea of these smaller notebooks, but they just don't work for me. Maybe it's my sprawling, childish handwriting. I always feel cramped trying to write in a small notebook. And I don't want to feel cramped when I write.

When I am home, my notebook has an important if quiet place in my writing life. At odd moments I duck into my office to jot something down. When I travel, the role of my notebook expands. At this moment I am writing in my notebook during a flight from Minneapolis to Boston. But it doesn't matter where I am. My office at home is my favorite place to write, but I've found that this notebook is all the place I need. My notebook is plenty big enough to conjure up all the concentric circles of my writing world—earth, home, office, desk, page, passage, sentence, word, and the impulse behind the word.

2

What Moves You?
What Matters?

Just at the lacy edge of the sea, a dolphin's skull. Recent, but
perfectly clean. And entirely beautiful. I held it in my hands, I
was so excited I was breathless. What will I do?

Mary Oliver

It was sunny and warm in New Hampshire the morning my
mother was scheduled for heart bypass surgery in Dallas. I was
hanging clothes out to dry when I happened to glance at my
watch: 11 A.M. New Hampshire time, which meant 9 A.M. Dallas time. My mother's surgery had begun at 8 A.M., and I knew
enough about bypass surgery to know that the surgeons typically
stop the heart to work on it. So at that moment while I was
busy hanging wet shirts on a clothesline my mother's heart was,
in all likelihood, stopped. I left the shirts, went inside, and began to write:

The Morning Mom's Heart Was Stopped
The morning Mom had bypass surgery I wrote a little but I
couldn't much concentrate so I cleaned up the kitchen, did a
laundry and hung it out on the clothesline. I pinned up the
shirts and imagined the surgeon's expensive hands, how he
would pin off her arteries and connect them to the heart-lung
machine. For an hour or two her heart would be stopped.
Stopped—the metronome I heard even inside her womb.
Stopped—the beating that filled my ears while I dozed at her
breast. Stopped—while the surgeon tried to work what im-

provements could be made. The wet shirts flashed in the spring sun. A breeze sprang up and filled the shirts with invisible torsos that swelled. And vanished.

If I want to write movingly I must first pay attention to what moves me. I must be connected to it: I must be *fused*. That's what the notebook is for. It gives you a roomy space to record and explore what amazes, delights, disgusts, or appalls you.

> Took Joseph (his six-month birthday) to the walk-in photo studio at Wal-Mart. The photographer looked like she was no more than twenty-five.
>
> "I've got some great props," she said with a smile. "Take off his shirt."
>
> First she photographed him in a little bathtub complete with soap and rubber ducky. Next she had him wearing a helmet, holding a nerf football. After that she took a picture of him with a baseball glove and cap. By now Joseph had had just about enough.
>
> "Just one more," she begged. She put a cowboy hat on his head. And then she gave him the gun. Toy pistol. Instinctively he put it in his mouth.
>
> "Isn't that the cutest?" she asked, grinning. I didn't know what to say.

Later this entry would spark a number of questions that would, in turn, lead to more writing. What symbols define a man in this society? a woman? What props would the photographer have used if Joseph were a Josephine?

Notebooks give you a place to freeze moments, insights, or stories in which you are directly involved. But you can go beyond that and use it to record striking things that involve people around you.

> B. [Black NYC teacher] told me about a music teacher who tried to discourage her from playing the flute. Your lips, he said, are too thick. "After that I was determined to play the flute," she told me in a low voice. "I practiced. I mastered it. And then I abandoned it."

11

The power of this story lies partly in the particular way B. told it to me, the suppressed fury in those three short sentences: *I practiced. I mastered it. And then I abandoned it.*

I was moved in a similar way after my wife, JoAnn, gave birth to our youngest son in a planned home birth with midwife, husband, children, and assorted relatives in attendance. This sounds chaotic; in fact it was remarkably calm and joyous. Joseph weighed ten pounds four ounces at birth. Afterward JoAnn lay in bed while her mother gave her a sponge bath.

> **JoAnn:** I found myself paying close attention to how she did it. The strokes, the pressure, how she moved from one part of me to another. It struck me that one day I might be doing the same thing for her.

JoAnn's words compressed years of time. When she said them I felt an inner stillness pass through me, a voice that told me: *Write it down.* This notebook entry may turn out to be no more than a poignant story but it sure feels like the seed for a larger piece of writing.

Often we are moved when we least expect it. One morning I was working in a junior high school, conducting a poetry workshop with a group of teachers. I was looking forward to hearing teachers share their own poetry. But first I asked them to reflect on their earliest memories of writing poetry in school.

"Funny thing is I used to be crazy about poetry," one woman said. "I loved it. Wrote and illustrated a whole book of my poems. Around that time we were having some work done on our house. Workers had to open up one wall and my daddy had the idea that we should all put something into that wall. You know, like a time capsule. Well, wouldn't you know I put in my book of poems. The workers closed up the wall. Six months later Dad got an unexpected promotion and we had to move. That was it."

"What happened?" I asked her. She shrugged.

"I stopped writing poetry. Just stopped. It's almost like I walled up whatever talent I once had." She laughed sadly. "You can't imagine how many times I've thought about going back to that house—which we don't even own anymore—and ripping open that wall to find my book of poems."

This is the kind of haunting story that winds up tucked into the pages of my notebook. This woman's love of poetry, stopped years ago. The nagging thought that bashing open that wall and holding the physical book of poems might somehow help her uncover the knack she once had for writing poetry.

I recognize myself in this woman's story because not every part of me survived the journey from childhood to the man I am today. Many parts of myself—the athlete, the visual artist—got lost or walled up in transit. So many things became too painful to care about, and so I hid them away in some forgotten place. It's intriguing to think that they might exist even now, buried but intact, like that book of poetry.

Your writer's notebook gives you a safe place to ask: *What really matters? What haunts me? What in my life, in this world, do I never want to forget?* Your notebook is an open invitation to care again about the world, and to bring those concerns into the full light of consciousness.

3

The Language Angels

In a recent interview the poet Sharon Olds said:

> We have a choice about what we write. We can write about anything. But I think that when we write that which turns out to have any strength in it, any language that we like, anything we want to show anyone else—we don't choose those subjects. They are just what matters most to us, and we didn't make ourselves. We didn't conceive or bear ourselves and we didn't invent our experiences. The poetry that we think works well enough to show each other comes from memory, thought, vision, imagination, history, whatever. It comes to us intensely enough that the language angels who fly around the room looking for places to land are drawn to this room where someone is, I don't know, trying to do something true.

I am struck by this passage, the image of "language angels" circling around and looking for a place to land. Sharon Olds's words conjure up the image of the Muse herself, that unpredictable goddess who taps a writer on the shoulder and breathes inspiration into the soul. I have always tended to write off this idea as charming and quaint, a romanticized conception of the creative process. I prefer a more plebian vision of the process: get up, pack your lunchbox, and it's off to work you go. Yet there have been a few rare times when I have felt the presence of wings followed by the sweet breath of inspiration.

One morning I woke up feeling alert and energized. And *fertile*. In my head I sensed the kicking presence of poetry, not just one or two poems but a whole series of love poems packed into my head, rich and dense as the seeds of a pomegranate. Before I lost them I jumped up, opened my notebook, and began to scribble down titles, lines, images. Later that day I began to write in earnest; the poems came in a flood. It took only three weeks to complete all the poems for *I Am Wings: Poems About Love*.

What happened? A secret transfer of wisdom from deep unconsciousness to my conscious mind? Some mystical gift channeled through me? I don't understand. All I know is that when it came time to write, the poems came quickly, easily, and required very little tinkering. Such gifts don't happen very often. But maybe they would be less rare if I were more ready to receive them.

Suzanne Gardinier is a poet and novelist. She has been keeping a journal since she was fourteen. One morning while visiting an art gallery with a friend she saw a statue of a woman. Her journal entry shows how profoundly it affected her:

> We talked with Morgan . . . and he took us in the back to show us something he'd bought on a trip to Ohio, a statue covered with a piece of plastic—the minute he unveiled it G. and I had tears in our eyes, as they met the eyes of this woman in wood, with her boy child held at her hip, clinging to her. There is no way I can describe her face here, the intensity of her gaze, her mouth closed and the corners pulled down—but I will never be the same after seeing her. See me, I heard. See my long days for other people's pleasure. See how my dress hangs down and my feet are bare. See the girl I was, who grew into this fierce woman. See the hard road I walked, the road my son has all ahead of him. Look in my eyes and tell me how you have kept the compact of sisters. Here I am.

At the time Suzanne was working on *The Seventh Generation*, a novel set in 1810. In the book's first section there is a character named Hannah Miller who bears a child after being raped by a white man. (Hannah is subsequently hanged.) Hannah is befriended by Mary Jones, a Welsh-descended woman in eastern Pennsylvania. You can see the direct impact of the journal entry in this excerpt from the novel:

The day before at Chapel Mary could not shake the smell of the burning city; she had stepped out onto the road grateful for the remnants of winter, the bare trees, the chill in the wind, the scraps of snow. She had shifted restless Benjamin and had turned and looked back over her shoulder, where the land fell away down the slope to Doe Run; stalking the grass ditch was an egret, the first she had seen since the late autumn, its still white bulk floating on still black legs, fixing her with a yellow sideways stare. She hummed the morning's last hymn. She would have no animal messengers. But that night Hannah came and stood by the bed, in a plain tow dress and bare feet, carrying a pale child in one arm. What is it? Mary asked, the question of the egret's curved neck. Look at my dress, Hannah had said. Look at my dress hang. Look at my feet. Look at the road I walked, the road my daughter has before her. Look at my eyes and tell me how you have kept the compact of sisters.

Your notebook can help you live in a state of creative readiness: to be sensitive to ideas and inspiration the way a piece of photographic paper is sensitive. That's one way I envision my notebook: alive to even the barest suggestion of light.

4

Thirteen Drops of Wine

Not long after noon—he could tell by the thin shadow of the
shutter.

F. Scott Fitzgerald

Morning. Laundry time. I stood by the washing machine, buttoning a dirty shirt before I threw it in. With a bemused look,
JoAnn watched me perform this ritual.

"I've always wanted to ask you," she said. "Why do you do
that?"

"Dunno," I shrugged. "You *have* to button shirts up before
you wash them, right? They hold their shape better that way."

JoAnn just looked at me.

"That's what Marian used to say," I added lamely.

"Oh," JoAnn replied, letting the name of my ex-wife hang in
the air between us. I stood there, feeling a little stupid, slowly
feeding the buttons through the slits in the shirtfront. For a few
seconds I fell into a sort of trance. In some peculiar way buttoning up that dirty shirt conjured up the all-but-forgotten world of
my relationship with Marian. In my notebook I wrote a very
short entry about this as a placeholder until I could come back
to it:

buttoning up dirty shirt—Marian

William Stafford once referred to a detail as a "golden
thread." The poet Robert Bly explains: "[Stafford] believes that
whenever you set a detail down in language, it becomes the end

of a thread . . . and every detail—the sound of the lawn mower, the memory of your father's hands, a crack you once heard in lake ice, the jogger hurtling herself past your window—will lead you to amazing riches."

For Stafford any detail will work, but he warned that many writers pull the golden thread too hard and make it break. The trick, Stafford suggested, is not to pull the thread but to *follow* it and see where it takes you.

A few weeks after writing my entry about buttoning the dirty shirt I started a poem based on this idea. I tried to follow the thread of buttoning back to its source and dredge up all the connected ideas I could remember. The sterile, "buttoned up" quality of our failed two-and-a-half-year marriage. An overemphasis on housework, clean floors, neatly ironed shirts. But buttoning also made me think of unbuttoning. And that brought the early passion into unexpected clarity. Here's where the thread finally took me:

Relic
I'll button this shirt
before it gets washed,
a useful habit picked up
from my first wife.
"They hold shape better
that way," she'd say,
and as it turns out
in this earthly matter
she was dead right.

I button it slowly down:
first spring, first touch,
the calm thrill of hands
undressing me without light
when each button blossomed
at the slightest touch
as warm fingertips startle

seeds of the touch-me-not
to spring open and apart.

The buttoned up shirt
gets tossed in the wash.
I turn the machine on.
The shirt writhes twice,
dives underwater,
disappears.

Writing puts you in a state of "constant composition," and this is particularly true of writing in a notebook. Regular notebook writing acts as a wakeup call, a daily reminder to keep all your senses alert. This starts a cycle that reinforces itself. Writing down small details gets you in the habit of seeking out the important small things in your world. These details in turn often lead you to new material you never knew you had.

In any piece of writing there is a "food chain" between the most general themes and the most concrete details. Skilled writers find a way to stay low (specific) on that food chain. I keep running into this idea and rethinking it. I used to believe that writers begin by coming up with broad topics or themes and proceed to dig up the supporting details and concrete nuggets that give their writing authenticity, telling particulars that illuminate the themes they want to explore.

Maybe it works that way for certain writers. But it's usually just the opposite with me. More often I stumble onto the detail first, take note of it in some way, and follow the detail as William Stafford describes. For me, "following the detail" happens over the course of writing a series of drafts. There is an element of mystery here, because during this process I discover what the poem is about.

I often use my notebook to record telling details, those tiny particulars that dramatically reveal a human situation. Here are several such entries. Any one of these details might later yield something worth pursuing.

What a control freak he is! The latest thing is that he has written the names of family members on the bottom of every item in the house. That way there will be no confusion or argument as to who inherits what after he dies.

Found a rusty cull rack in the pile of junk Mom was throwing out. Reminded me of digging clams with Bob. I decided to keep it.

Bill and his daughter Jen are forever misunderstanding eachother. When he asked what she wanted for her eighteenth birthday party he distinctly heard Jen say: "A cake." But the day before the party Jen insisted she said "A keg." She threw a fit when he wouldn't let her have one.

Spent the weekend with Al and Vickie. He works the early shift at the factory—she gets up every morning at 4:30 A.M. to fix him bacon and eggs. "I'm done doing that," she told us one night after he'd gone to sleep. "You think on his days off he gets up early to make *me* hot oatmeal before *I* go off to school? That'll be the day!" She sounded fiery and righteous as we all headed off to bed. But at 4:30 in the morning I was awoken by a strong and bewitching aroma. Frying bacon.

Details matter. In a poem, essay or story, a powerful detail allows the reader to understand the emotional drama. And it gives the reader plenty of space to enter into the world of the text. When we read a piece of writing it is often the apparently irrelevant detail we remember, even more than brilliant argument or lyrical language.

My notebook is full of such details but I don't collect them indiscriminately. I tend to look for small bits that embody a feeling or idea beyond themselves:

I finished the bottle of chardonnay. The waitress came by and poured the last bit into my glass. "Did you know," she asked, "that in an empty bottle there are still thirteen drops of wine?"

The thirteen drops of wine remaining in an empty wine bottle appeals to me because it might present an apt metaphor for those moments when we feel utterly empty but still have, or hope we have, a tiny bit in reserve.

Here's another example. At a college reuinion I reintroduced myself to a former classmate. After a few pleasantries, she lowered her eyes and told me that her husband had recently drowned on a lake in Minnesota.

"He fell through the ice, managed to pull himself out, and fell through again," she told me in a hushed voice.

I retold this story to several people. Each time I found myself repeating the part about how he had been able to pull himself out of one hole only to fall through a second time. The fact that her husband had drowned would seem to render this part of the story irrelevant. Or does it? Maybe a haunting detail like this is the most important part because of the way it lodges in our consciousness and makes the story impossible to forget.

5

Triggers: Lines, Bits, Lists, Questions

New York on a summer night. How many lights are burning? A man sits on the front steps of the public library wearing no coat and no shoes and a dark felt hat. His shoes are beside him on the marble step.

John Cheever

In *Turning Life into Fiction* Robin Hemley writes: "A journal is essentially the place we store triggers—things that have caught our attention and started our imaginations rolling."

Part of me wants to rebel against the idea of shoehorning the notebook into such a practical, calculated role in the writing life. But Hemley's idea makes a great deal of sense because the notebook is an enormously practical writing tool. It is a bank account you will dip into again and again. It gives you a regular place to record whatever you think might be a catalyst for a sustained piece of writing. And often what you record is nothing more than a glint, line, gesture, or fragment.

Writers' notebooks are filled with what Joan Didion calls "string too short to be saved" yet are too important to throw away: the writerly instinct is to hang onto them. While rummaging through his attic Donald Hall found a box his mother had carefully labeled "string too short to be saved." He used this phrase for the title of a memoir about his childhood. Your notebook can work as a place to keep these fragments alive until you're ready to put them to use.

You might be impressed at the way I have organized this chapter into clearly marked sections: Odd Facts, Lines, Lists, Questions, and so on. Of course, this regimentation is an outrageous fiction; my notebooks are about as systematic and organized as the kitchen junk drawer in our house, and other writers have commented about the random nature of their notebooks. The divisions in this chapter are for the purposes of discussion only. If you are interested in a closer approximation of my actual notebook, mix these entries vigorously after you finish the chapter.

Odd Facts

If you could find a large enough ocean to hold it, Saturn would *float* (radio info)

from Anselm Hollo's notebook

The notebook provides an ideal place to hide your stash. And along with everything else, a writer's stash usually includes nuggets of indisputable truth drawn from history, astronomy, biochemistry. These facts can be odd, astonishing, comical or intriguing. Writers tend to collect a juicy fact even when there is no apparent use for it.

"There does not seem to be . . . any point in my knowing for the rest of my life that, during 1964, 720 tons of soot fell on every square mile of New York City," Joan Didion writes in *Slouching Towards Bethlehem*, "yet there it is in my notebook, labeled 'FACT.' "

The facts I gather in my notebook go beyond themselves to reveal some important or intriguing facet of the world. For example: *A solar year is the amount of time it takes for our sun to make one full rotation around our galaxy*. I recently jotted this fact into a notebook even though it has no practical purpose in my writing *at this time*. I simply loved the sound of this phrase, *solar year*, the cool way it puts the passage of earthly time into galactic perspective. A fact like this might one day serve as a catalyst or trigger for a larger piece of writing. Or it might not. I figure that even if it doesn't, my life is richer for knowing it.

> Astronomers have increased their estimate of the known galaxies in the universe from ten billion to fifty billion. (*New York Times* 1/18/96)

> The average person has forty moles on their body. (dermatology pamphlet)

> Some aphasic children cannot be taken to the supermarket for the impressions made on their brains by the lights, colors, sounds, the cold of the air-conditioning, the clatter and chatter. The kids panic because their brains can't sort out the difference between important and unimportant sense stimuli.

In a recent talk Richard Allington mentioned that in U.S. schools we spend an average of $52 per child per year on dittoes. This fact intrigued me (could this money be better spent?), so I wrote it in my notebook. What about you? What have you recently read that make you put down your coffee and reread to make sure you got it right? What facts fascinate you?

Questions

Some years ago I met a young woman named Monica on the train to New York City. Monica was a model for the Ford Agency. She had luminous skin and pale gray eyes so huge I couldn't help complimenting her on them. She readily agreed with me. "I'm pretty strong through the eyes," she admitted coolly, like a baseball pitcher describing his best strikeout pitch. On the train men and women kept glancing over to stare at her. Later I wrote about this in my notebook:

> What would it be like to be so astonishingly beautiful? How will this girl ever have a normal encounter with the world?

Many writers have remarked that their best writing begins with a nagging question or issue, big or small. Your notebook is a place to pursue these questions but you can't pursue them unless you write them down. I use my notebook to write down questions, especially the difficult ones with no easy answers.

Why is it that so many smart women are attracted to narcissistic men?

Why is it so hard to tell him I love him the way I tell my wife, the way I tell my children?

Writing down questions is no quirk of mine. In fact, if you crack open the published notebooks of other writers you'll see the same thing.

Why do we pull a sheet over the faces of the dead? Why do we cover our eyes instead of just closing them when we're afraid?

Sharon Bryan

Who would tell the mockingbird his song is frivolous, since it lacks words?

Mary Oliver

What is it you wonder or daydream about during the quiet moments of the day? What are the questions that haunt the edges of your consciousness? Your notebook gives you a forum for the unresolved questions and arguments that take place inside you. *An argument with another person leads to rhetoric; an argument with yourself can lead to poetry.*

Odds and Ends

Most of what goes into a notebook defies description. Labeling it, well, *stuff*, is about as close as you get. If your notebook is like mine, it will fill up with stuff you can't quite live without:

Joseph (2-1/2) insists that I cut his ice cream into pieces he can manage with his spoon.

In our lifetime we may see the end of the shellfish industry (overheard on radio)

In the '50s if you saw a car with one headlight missing you reached over and kissed your girlfriend.

Sheila irons everything: towels, sheets, even paper money. "I don't do anything above a twenty," she once confided to me. "That's as high as I go."

Lists

Writers are inveterate list makers. I list favorite words (I love the dinosaur-like bulk of *gargantuan*) and names (*Boutros Boutros-Ghali* is my current favorite). Creating a list has the feel of doing something practical: gathering evidence, accumulating knowledge, making a start. And a list can segue into a workable plan for a larger writing project.

You might keep a variety of lists in your notebooks: things to do, ideas for poems, old boyfriends, an aunt's annoying gestures. Here is a list taken from the notebook of Philip Booth:

Names of Islands:

Pond	Thrumcap
Hog	Ram
Butter	Sheep
Sprucehead	The Virgin's Breasts
Horsehead	Pumpkin
Colthead	Two Bush

And one from the notebooks of mystery writer Raymond Chandler:

Titles:
The Man with the Shredded Ear
All Guns Are Loaded
Return From Ruin
The Man Who Loved the Rain
The Corpse Came in Person
Law Is Where You Buy It
Sit with Me While I Dream (autobiography?)

They Only Murdered Him Once
Too Late for Smiling
Deceased When Last Seen
The Quiet Ivories (piano used to hide a body á la Stevenson)
The Black-Eyed Blond
Quick, Hide the Body
Goodnight and Goodbye

A practical suggestion: important lists can get lost in a crowded notebook so beware of jamming too much onto any one page. Some writers leave a blank page opposite the page with written entries. Try to leave enough white space around your entries so they can breathe, so you can find them when you reread and react if you feel the urge to do so.

Lines and Insights

Her unselfishness came in pretty small packages well-wrapped.

F. Scott Fitzgerald

To me the one-liner is the coup d'état of writing, the reverse slam dunk, the impossible cross-court volley that nicks the line and makes the spectators gasp in awe. I'm a sucker for a great line: the brevity, the wit, the way some writers can skewer a complex idea in a stylish sentence or two. A fine line can reduce me to woofing and applauding like an enthusiastic circus seal.

Nothing answered me, not even the stand-in for an echo.

Raymond Chandler

Time is the school in which we learn that time is the fire in which we burn.

Delmore Schwartz

It is a vulgar error to suppose that America was ever discovered. It was merely detected.

Oscar Wilde

27

Writers use their notebooks to collect lines from other writers as well as to record their own. (During conversation novelist Victor Hugo used to take out his notebook to jot down some brilliant remark *he* happened to make!) Dip into most writer's notebooks and you'll find a weakness for the zinger, aphorism, epigram, barbed comment. Writers collect wonderful lines, partly in hopes of one day using them, partly for the sheer pleasure of savoring masterful language.

Occasionally I'll come up with a pretty good line, completely separate from any longer work of fiction or poetry.

> Her downcast eyes jerked at me as I walked past, as if I'd hit some delicate trip wire laid by her psyche.

It has been my experience that a line like this will bounce around in my head until it finally fades away. But I can give it a home in my notebook. Many writers jot down suggestive lines they think might yield more at a later time.

Lines, ideas:
The smell of oil and gas . . .
Bob's strutting skinny walk . . .
The lake bulging . . .

Fish nibbling at the bait of the moon resting on the surface . . .

Vern Rutsala

You might think of your notebook as a "holding pattern" for intriguing or unfinished lines until you're ready to bring them in for a landing. This is equally true when it comes to insights. I use my notebook to jot down insights about the world, either original or overheard.

> Whoever loves least in a relationship wields the most power.

During a plane ride I sat next to a man, a stranger, who made this troubling statement during a long conversation. I knew I'd want to write more about it later so I made sure to write it down. Often I hear an insight in a fragment from the TV, radio,

28

or other mass media. I heard these insights about mothers on the radio:

> Mothers love their sons and raise their daughters.

> A mother can take care of nine children, but when she gets old nine children aren't enough to take care of one mother.

The echo of a line is often more important than the line itself. Lines like these start me thinking about motherhood, about my mother and her nine children, about . . . .

The triggers you collect can hibernate in your notebook until you feel like waking them up. But there is nothing foolproof about this process. Often you'll get seized by a terrific idea only to find your enthusiasm has dried up along with the the ink used to write it down. Expect that. At other times you will experience the excitement of reencountering an idea well worth pursuing. These occasions, however rare, make the whole thing worthwhile.

I think of this process as putting ingredients into a pot for soup and knowing from experience that it will taste good today but better tomorrow. And even better the day after that.

6

Breathing In the
Physical World

*Cormorant on a lake stump. A most flexible and ever-moving
neck, velvet black back & large spread wings with gray tatters
like the old coat of an elegant aging gentleman. He points with
his neck—I suppose constantly searching for food. Japanese
grace and absurd balance. It seems his wings would ache from
holding them outstretched like that. The way some people do.*

Liz Rosenberg

Anyone who writes has a real life and a textual life. The writer's
notebook is situated squarely between those two worlds. You
might think of your notebook as a strong thin membrane between the life you live and the life you try to create on the page.
A permeable membrane that allows plenty of breathing back
and forth.

The physical world has a direct impact on what you write in
your notebook. While talking on the phone, hand on your hip,
you notice your three-year-old daughter standing in exactly the
same pose. You write this down. This is the simplest way writers
use their notebooks. But it works the other way, too. Once you get
in the habit of writing in your notebook you'll find yourself paying
closer attention to what is going on in the world around you.

In Hilo, Hawaii, I'm walking at night beneath an enormous
banyan tree. The tree has a dizzying network of branches and a
trunk at least twelve feet in diameter. It is night but there is
enough light for me to look up and see roots dangling from the

branches. Beyond, in the breaks between the limbs, I can glimpse the stars. I'm exhausted from ten hours of flying but when I get back to my hotel room I flip open my notebook to record the moment:

> Walking at night beneath a banyan tree. My first impression is that whoever built this tree did a lousy job. For one thing it's much too big, should have been subdivided into four or five trees. The trunk looks like a bunch of thin sticks loosely bundled together, a trunk some kids might put together. And what are those roots doing up in the air instead of in the soil where they belong? Beyond them I can see bits of light which makes me think: it's high time the wandering stars finally put down some roots . . .

Much of my writing has been rooted in close observation of the physical world. At the end of writing days I usually reward myself with a four-mile walk here in Durham. This loop inspired a book of poems, *Ordinary Things*, but it didn't happen all at once. For a long time I walked like a ghost through that lovely scenery because the crowded landscape in my head— worries, ambitions, nagging things to do—prevented me from being present. I took that walk a dozen times before I really began to tune in to the trees and stone walls. After that I started noticing the smell of horses and how the smell gets stronger on rainy days. I saw white birches against the blue sky and freshly pruned apple trees that reminded me of gnarled old men caught in a ludicrous ballet.

It is difficult to observe the world if we are preoccupied with other things. But we can learn to do so. (Thich Nhat Hanh, a Vietnamese Buddhist, has written an eloquent book called *The Miracle of Mindfulness* that speaks to this issue.) I find that there are plenty of times when I have to gently tell myself, *Shut up and pay attention to what is going on.*

> The black-eyed Susans were stunning all through August and September, black eyes brilliantly set off against the yellow petals. Now in October the flowers have withered and fallen off.

Just the pupils are left, Prozac stare, a corpse whose eyes nobody has gotten around to closing.

The diaries of Virginia Woolf contain many long passages in which Woolf opens herself up to some phenomenon of the natural world. At one point she writes a three-page description of the aurora borealis. Here she painstakingly describes a summer storm:

> A violent rain storm on the pond. The pond is covered with little white thorns; spring up and down: the pond is bristling with leaping white thorns, like the thorns on a small porcupine; bristles; then black waves; cross it; black shudders; and the little water thorns are white; a helter skelter rain and the elms tossing it up and down; the pond overflowing on one side; lily leaves tugging; the red flower swimming about; one leaf flapping; then completely smooth for a moment; then prickled; thorns like glass; but leaping up and down incessantly; a rapid smirch of a shadow. Now light from the sun; green and red; shiny; the pond a sage green; the grass brilliant green; red berries on the hedges; the cows very white; purple over Asheham.

Nature is inspiring but that's not the only way to get inspired. Writers learn to breathe in the world wherever they are: in a bathtub, bed, church, Salvation Army. Writer Alicia Ostriker observed passengers boarding her plane and jotted this entry in her notebook:

> People seen on plane: a couple of old Jewish people right out of Tell Me A Riddle—the husband short, stout & bouncy, saying "God bless you" to the flight attendants, the wife's face a map of brown wrinkles; blind; needing help out of the wheelchair into the plane, & help up the aisle—given by her daughter, middle-aged woman in K-Mart clothes (no not quite).

The entries cited so far are fairly long; many writers use much shorter bursts of observation. Franz Kafka's diaries contain many brief entries:

The onlookers go rigid when the train goes past.

A band of little golden beads around a tanned throat.

As you start paying closer attention to the physical world, try to push beyond the sight into the other less glamorous senses: smell, taste, touch. I like how this notebook entry by Fitzgerald sets a mood of expectation and understated suspense by describing a familiar sound:

> Car description on quiet night, padded hush of tires, quiet tick of a motor running idle at curb.

Some writers give themselves brief assignments to stretch their ability to describe the physical world. Each house has its particular smell—*describe the difference between one house's smell and another's. Describe the unique smell of school children.* When you challenge yourself like this, try to be as specific as possible. For instance: *describe the smell of children coming in from a rainy playground.*

Describing a character is the hardest thing for me in my writing, so in my notebook I often push myself to describe hands, a face, a telling gesture:

> The dreamy look she got reaching into the bag of prunes, trying to find the softest one . . .

> Joseph's peculiar habit of cocking his head and nodding as he speaks makes him appear knowing and adult. My little professor.

As we live in the physical world the brain works nonstop to sort and make sense of incoming perceptions: *Oh, that sounds like Dad.* Or: *That's not a looming giant—that's just a tree.* In my notebook I try hard to capture the raw perceptions, those uncertain moments when I'm not yet sure what I'm noticing:

> A silhouetted figure walking in the distant field. Can't tell at first if he's walking toward me or away.

> Walked at 4 P.M. today. Cold, overcast skies. Reached the highway and spotted a pale globe trying to fight through the winter

33

clouds just above the tree line. The sun, I guessed, but it gave off so little light and warmth I half-thought it might've been the moon.

My first day at college. Went to my empty dorm room and promptly fell asleep. Woke up feeling disoriented, lonely. When I went outside the light was murky. Kids were hurrying across the green. The clock on the belltower said 7 but I had absolutely no idea if it was 7 at night or 7 in the morning.

The notebook is a place to record honest perceptions of and reactions to the physical world. You will want to record important specifics but you may also be tempted to move away from strict accuracy and begin to invent. Go for it! The impulse toward play begins immediately in many writers, from the initial act of breathing in the world and writing down a perception. Such play can take place through analogies, metaphor, puns, or personification. Many writers use their notebooks to play with images from the everyday world:

Purse as womb

Rita Dove

A porcelain cup overturned on a plate: an iridiscent igloo.

Rita Dove

Leaf-covered car: like driving a float in a fall parade.

Sharon Bryan

Other writers use their notebooks as sketchbooks where they draw what they encounter in the physical world. (If you intend to sketch you may want to get a notebook without lines.) A quick sketch is a fine way to capture an observed gesture, a grimace, the toys scattered on a lawn. I don't draw; I was one of those students who learned somewhere around fifth grade that I wasn't any good at art. Someday, I tell myself, I'll learn how to draw. Until that time I will have to paint my pictures with words as the poet Mary Oliver does in so many of her notebook entries:

Hundreds of gannets feeding just offshore, plunging, tufts of water rising with a white up-kick. Scary birds, long wings, very white, fearful-looking beaks. We opened the car windows and there was no sound but the sound of their wings rustling. They fed at three or four places, then were gone much farther out. We were at the right place at the right time.

7

Talk

---

*He was very funny when we woke up . . . asking if I wanted
him to go into town to get croissants. I said I would love a
croissant but I didn't want him to go to the trouble and he said,
it's all right, it's a "croiss" I'd gladly bear.*

Brenda Hillman

My kids' utterances are ingredients in a conversational soup.
They jabber at each other, flavoring each other's language, imi-
tating and contradicting, making alliances, demanding attention, trying to hold the floor, each one pushing his own slant on
the doings around the house. Even the baby wants in on the action. At the supper table Joseph announces: "I have an idea!"
then stops, amazed and delighted when everyone quiets down
to listen to him.

Me, too. Even now, with my kids at school, in the solitude of
my office, part of me is restless, lonely, wishing I were with a
friend at a bustling restaurant feasting on a steaming bowl of
gossip, hearsay, slang, story. I am ravenous for it. I wouldn't
even mind eating alone so long as I could be surrounded by people doing what people do best: talking.

My notebooks are chock-filled with talk. I must have devel-
oped this sweet tooth for conversation growing up in a big family where the First Amendment was alive and kicking, where
nobody ever shut up. I love human speech. Whenever someone
at a nearby restaurant table starts talking I get quiet so I can listen both to what they say and how they say it.

"It is the responsibility of writers to listen to gossip and pass it on," Grace Paley says. "It is the way all storytellers learn about life."

True. I believe that conversation is a crucial element when it comes to revealing character or conflict, when it comes to revealing the inner workings of a particular world. Learning both the music of spoken language and how to use this music are essential parts of the writer's craft. Dip into almost any notebook and you will find that the author has recorded a wealth of talk.

Slang

Most workplaces have a lexicon of slang words that name or describe the particulars of that world. When I worked as a tour leader the slang included:

pax—passenger
stag group—group composed solely of men
sked air—scheduled airline (as opposed to charter)
hots and colds—hot and cold hors d'oeuvres
plus plus—cost of service plus tax and gratuity

F. Scott Fitzgerald's notebooks had a section for slang words. Raymond Chandler also used his notebooks to list slang that later showed up in his mysteries. Chandler was interested in how slang differed from one world to the next.

Hard Talk:
Eel juice—liquor
Chicago lightning—gunfire

Hollywood Slang:
Jail break—time out to eat

San Quentin Prison Slang:
Croaker—doctor
Back door parole—die in prison

Slang acts as a verbal shorthand that signals membership in a closed world: police force, maintenance crew, nursing station, teaching staff. Using slang is a way of announcing, *I am an insider.* It creates a sense of community, keeps the outside world at bay, and speeds up communication between the people who use it. You can use your notebook to record slang wherever you hear it:

studmuffin—good-looking boy
wicked—very, as in *wicked hot*
sweet—kid's slang for cool, great (a sweet car)
spendy—slang for expensive, a spendy restaurant

Colorful Language

One winter a bunch of friends and I rented a house in Grantham, New Hampshire. The weather on the first day was clear but very cold; my friend Mark Mittelman balked when I suggested we all take a walk on the lake.

"This is a Windex kind of day," Mark deadpanned. "It's way too cold to go outside. I say we get out the Windex and clean the windows. That way we can look outside all we want but stay inside where it's nice and warm."

In my family we still joke about a *Windex kind of day* when the weather gets cold and blustery. Mark has a knack of coming up with sayings like that—many have ended up in my notebooks.

> Phone message from Mark, after hearing that JoAnn was pregnant: "Congratulations! I hear you two are going to be taking a splash in the gene pool! Mazeltov!"

My notebooks also contain lots of surprising things my children say. One editor recently cautioned me that readers don't have much patience for "toddlerspeak." Maybe so, but I'll never forget how Garp's son talked about the "undertoad" (undertow) or "gradual school" (graduate school) in John Irving's novel *The World According to Garp.* Children, who are far less socialized than adults, remind me again and again of the delightful possibilities that reside in language. Writers like the poet Naomi Shihab Nye record their children's expressions, sayings that often suggest a poem or story. This recent entry involves my five-year-old:

> While I'm kneeling with Robert, helping him put on his boots, he caresses the bald spot on top of my head and exclaims: "Hey, Daddy, it's like the sun is breaking through the clouds!"

Verbal flourishes show up anywhere people open their mouths. Recently I was visiting a friend whose daughter is a senior in high school. A woman from the neighborhood strolled past one evening and stopped to comment on my friend's daughter, to rave about the girl's grace, beauty, and long legs.

"Your daughter," the woman said, "has legs up to her eyeballs."

At a restaurant my brother Tom once asked the waiter to put enough black pepper on his salad "so it looks like a coal miner sneezed on it." I recorded this expression in my notebook and later used it in a novel—*Spider Boy*.

Writing down spoken language requires careful listening and a willingness to be surprised. Nabokov, novelist and butterfly expert, once overheard a young child pointing out a "flutter-by"—a word he delighted in as an improvement over butterfly. The trick is to listen not to what you think someone is trying to say but to the words that are actually spoken, even if those words are ungrammatical. Did the boy say that math class is "more fun than English" or "funner than English"?

My notebook also gets flavored by the occasional earthy expression people are speak at unguarded moments. Off-color remarks can be crude or offensive. Still, they are are remarkable for their candor; they have a way of cutting through the facade of polite society to pinpoint exactly what's going on. Here are a few examples.

One morning on a tour to Nassau, the Bahamas, one of the group members pulled me aside and motioned at a group of five husbands drinking coffee.

"Most of these guys can't wait for their wives to go off shopping in the morning so they can hit the can like they really want to."

I once brought a hundred accountants, all stags, on a tour to Germany. Seven days of booze and bad money jokes. One day while riding on a bus from a restaurant back to the hotel I overheard two of my tourists talking. This exchange typified the entire tour.

First man: "Do you still make love to your wife?"
Second man (*laughing*): "Make love to my wife? Sure I do. We make love about once every fiscal period."
First man (*singing loudly*): "Let's get fis-cal. I wanna get fis-cal . . . ."

When we hear earthy expressions or slang, we are encountering talk in its most natural state. Any writer who hopes to create believable dialogue, dramatic scenes, and characters who speak in an authentic voice needs to learn the nuances of such speech.

You don't have to go to the trouble of recording an entire conversation in your notebook. The entry can be a short one— *Mark: Windex kind of day.* Get in, write it down, and get out. Write down just enough to rouse your memory when you reread it.

A Spoken Slice of Life

This is the final exchange between the pilots on the Air Florida flight that crashed into the Potomac on January 13, 1982. The remarks were recorded on the tape in the black box found in the wreckage and got printed in the *New York Times*. I was struck by the professionalism of the crew and, at the very end, the men's acknowledgment of their fate. I copied this dialogue into my notebook.

First Officer: "God, look at that thing . . . that doesn't seem right, does it?"
Captain: "Yes it is, there's eighty."

First Officer: "Naw, I don't think that's right . . . ah, maybe it is."
Captain: "Hundred and twenty."
First Officer: "I don't know."
Captain: "Vee One. Easy. Vee Two. Forward, forward . . . come on, forward . . . just barely climb."
Crew Member: "Stalling, we're [falling]."
First Officer: "Larry, we're going down, Larry."
Captain: "I know it." (*Impact*)

Writers are drawn to any real talk that unveils a world: its emotional undercurrents, conflicts, hopes, tensions, and frustrations. You can capture this in many ways—by writing down a single sentence, a brief exchange between people, or a more detailed scene. In the following notebook entry John Cheever records the discourse between himself and his wife over the course of a day.

Our conversation goes, by my account, like this. Me: Good morning. She: Good morning (faintly). Me: May I have the egg on the stove? She: You know I never eat eggs. "Goodbye," I say, after breakfast. (Silence.) "Would you like a drink?" I ask at five. "Yes, please." "This book is very interesting," I say. "It must be," she sighs. I chat during dinner, but she remains silent. These are the words we exchange during a day.

You can train yourself to listen to talk wherever you go—supermarket, church, doctor's office. Since I spend a great deal of time visiting schools I often overhear talk between teachers in the staff room, dialogue laced with frustration, fatigue, and a grim survival humor.

"The full moon was yesterday," a teacher says. "The wolf moon. It really affects people. I used to work in an institution. I know."

"Used to work in an institution!" another teacher laughs. "Used to?!"

"You can tell when the barometer changes by how the kids react," the first teacher says. "They go berserk."

"Do you have a barometer in your class?"
"Yeah. Twenty-eight of them."

On the train I met a woman who blurted out that her marriage had just ended. "Thirty-two years: poof! He left a note on the formica in the kitchen. I never knew he was unhappy. I never had an inkling." She must have repeated the same words—*I never had an inkling*—a dozen times.

I often return to an entry like this one to ruminate, expand, play. In this case the woman's spoken words suggested a poem:

inkling
I never had an inkling my marriage is
over thirty-two years do you believe
this my husband just left he left
a note on the kitchen formica I
never had an inkling I never
had an inkling and she kept
repeating those five words
in exactly that order until
the word *inkling* started
rattling like a chime in
a cold wind or ice
cubes tinkling
in a glass left
on a mirror
smashed
to tiny
b i t s

In certain respects notebook entries remind me of the "astronaut ice cream" my kids are so wild about. With all the moisture removed, the remaining ice cream is feather light and portable. Only the essentials—the flavor, the chalky feel—are left. In the same way, when you record something in your notebook you can leave out the fluff.

If you're writing in your notebook while you are tired or

rushed, you might be tempted to take a shortcut and write just a summary of the conversation. Beware! Usually, when recording a dramatic scene you can remove almost everything *except* the actual talk.

Talk is not an isolated element in writing but is tangled up with tension, voice, character, the poetry of surprise. As you tune into human speech you stumble onto bits of raw eloquence and great feeling. At times people speak in a way that is simply beautiful. My friend Doug Worthen described his ten-year-old son, Ben, like this:

> He's about five or six years old when he wakes up. He snuggles in bed, you know, sits on my lap. But as the day goes on he sort of gets older, eight, nine, ten. By mid-afternoon he's at least fifteen, arguing with me, telling me he wants to go to the mall or stay over a friend's house. At night he gets ready for bed and he wants me to lie with him after the light goes off and he starts getting younger again, eight, five, three. Finally he falls alseep.

8

The Echo of the Past

We forget all too soon the things we thought we could never forget. We forget the loves and betrayals alike, forget what we whispered and what we screamed, forget who we were.

Joan Didion

In late October 1974 my brother Bob was injured in a car wreck and rushed to the hospital. For four days he remained in critical condition while our family kept vigil. At first we found small reasons to hope, but as the days passed the realization slowly set in that we were going to lose him.

One night my mother came home early from the hospital. Exhausted, she flopped on the living room couch. My brothers and sisters and I drifted over to sit around her. My sister brought her a cup of tea. All at once, without any prompting, my mother began telling the stories of our births. Everyone had heard these stories before, but we listened now without speaking.

"Kathy, you arrived early for once," Mom said. "When I laid eyes on you, my God, you were the tiniest thing, five pounds something and perfect as a porcelain doll." She looked at me. "Ralphie, you were my first. When you were born I wanted to write you a letter, right then, to tell you how amazing it was, such a miracle to have your tiny hand in mine. . . ."

It was Robert Frost who said that often the most important gifts we receive as writers are gifts we're unaware of at the time. But we can train ourselves to go back to moments of crisis, discovery, or loss. We can unwall those memories and bring them to the light of consciousness. This is one of the most important ways I use my notebook.

"As we age," John Updike says, "we leave behind us a litter of old selves." Many writers use their notebooks to go back and re-visit the selves they have not quite left behind.

> I was a quiet baby my grandmother told me scary quiet with big eyes and two fingers tucked in my mouth.
>
> Dorothy Allison

> The memory of that icy time when our streets were frozen and high school kids played hockey on it under the streetlights. The strangeness of it, their long gliding moments, the quiet except for the sounds of the skates.
>
> Vern Rutsala

It is a human trait to be "borne ceaselessly into the past," and this is particularly true for writers. In his journals Cheever writes about "the galling loneliness of my adolescence, from which I do not seem to have completely escaped." Writers re-open old boxes, pick at old wounds, return to old themes and obsessions. Most of us find the past the steadiest, most reliable supplier of material for our work.

The memories that show up in my notebooks are a potpourri of poignant moments, everyday life, and recollected odd facts from the past:

> Feel and smell of Vicks VapoRub on my chest when I was little. . . .

> Going to Sunday mass in July, church so full of Cape Cod tourists you couldn't even get in, standing by the back door with Jesus on the inside and sweet summer outside.

> Just before supper the kids in our family would get down on our knees to "snick up" the floor: pick up tiny pieces of dirt and dust and lint. (Is *snick* a word? Why didn't we use the vacuum?)

> The morning Mom asked Dad if he'd like more bacon. "Sure," Dad said, winking at me. "Bacon's one of those things you never

get enough of." That sudden glimpse of my father as a man with his own wants and unsatisfied desires.

These entries summon the landscape of the childhood world I inhabited on the way to becoming a man. Your notebook is an invitation to return to this landscape, to touch base with all the old selves you left along the way.

You may find that in casting back into the past you pull up more fragments than intact memories. That's all right; write about these fragments as faithfully as you can. The inch of cream on the top of the bottle of milk that got delivered. The way your grandmother used to talk in her sleep after she had eaten lobster for dinner.

There was a place in the woods near my house where a flourescent light once broke; rumor had it that a quantity of deadly gas got released. For years afterward I held my breath, all the neighborhood kids did, running past that spot.

I try to pay particular attention to the memories I don't wholly understand (the summer of my sophomore year when I stopped combing my hair), what stirs up strong feelings. When I begin to write about a memory, I'm less interested in the general feeling of the memory than in whatever specifics I can recall.

> Moving day. In my head I said goodbye to our house, goodbye to our street. Before we got into the car I picked up a leaf, an ordinary leaf from the yard, and snuck it into the car with me. We drove for hours and hours and when we got to our new house I brought the leaf out of the car with me and let it fall onto the ground. It gave me a funny feeling to see the leaf from back home on the ground with those strange leaves in that new place. "Let's go look inside," Dad said. I followed him but I kept coming back to the car to check on the leaf. Then a kid from next door came over with a basketball and asked if I felt like playing. When I came back I looked for that leaf but I couldn't tell the old from the new.

Your notebook allows you to dredge up and examine past memories but it can also help you preserve memories from the present, serving as a scrapbook to collect artifacts from the world around you, items to which you suspect you'll want to return.

Your notebook might contain a teacher's note from the day-care center, a difficult letter you sent or received, tickets from a remarkable rock concert, the matchbook cover from the restaurant where you argued with your father. Later, when actual memory has faded, these objects have potent magic in summoning up the events connected to them.

Many writers like to include in their notebooks newspaper articles that pique their interest.

"I keep a lot of clippings in my journals," novelist Dorothy Allison says. "The clippings range from two-sentence notes I pull from articles, letters, and news reports to photos from various sources and even horoscopes clipped out of magazines."

In addition to artifacts, you can use words to fix a moment you suspect you'll want to remember and explore later:

> I arrive at a school where I am scheduled to work. Feel a dull throb in my chest—tell myself it's nothing more than heartburn. Blue skies. Up a grassy incline the forest announces itself with the alluring scent of wet fresh leaves on the ground. I want to scramble up (such inclines are meant to be scrambled up) to those decaying leaves, grab a fistful, drink in the moist smell. But my hands would get dirty, I'm wearing nice clothes and already late for my first class. I pull myself away from the scent, the dull ache, and hurry inside the school. Part of the machine—or a human being?

An entry like this one strives to capture a fleeting moment from present-day life. More than diary-like recounting of events, a notebook encourages you to delve deeper and describe the emotional landscape of the experience.

"*Remember what it was to me:* that is always the point," Joan Didion says of a writer's notebook. "*How it felt to be me:* that is getting closer to the truth about a notebook."

The past has a way of reverberating in the present. Seeing my kids at Christmas stirs up echoes of my own childhood Christmases. Being a father prompts memories of spending time with my father when I was a boy. And watching the birth of my son reminds me of that night my mother retold those birth stories while my brother lay at the edge of death.

A few weeks after Bob's funeral I wrote about that evening in a brief notebook entry. I didn't return to it right away. If my notebooks have taught me anything, they have taught me that it's okay—even necessary—to wait before writing further about an idea. A full decade would pass before I reread that entry. And when I did I found that I felt serene enough to write this poem.

Echo

Whenever somebody called for my father
I answered as well when I was a child
both proud and pleased that our shared name
could fit us both in one snug syllable,
only later awash in sullen dissynchrony
when I began to feel no more than his echo

or the echo of my mother, wizard of birth
spawning brothers, sisters, and me in
such sturdy succession it sometimes seems
we were born together, all holding hands.
As she aged I imagined the years
as cunning little animals, nocturnal,
treading her face at night while she slept
leaving footprints of lines and wrinkles.

When my fourth brother lay dying
she pulled us around like a favorite quilt
and told the separate stories of our births.
Like a lost bullbat or sounding whale
she bounced off our hearts this lone signal
and used the echo to somehow
find her way home.

9

Necessary Words

[Description of a man trying to read while sitting on the deck of a ship] *The inquisitive breeze would join in the reading and roughly finger the pages so as to discover what was going to happen next.*

Vladimir Nabokov

If we hope to write well, we have to learn from the men and women who have mastered our craft. We draw as close to them as they will allow and watch them at work. This is apprenticeship the old-fashioned way and I don't believe there's any way around it. We need to read and reread the finest writers we can find. We need to study and savor their language. And on occasion we might copy snatches of it into a notebook as a reminder of what language can do in the hands of a skilled writer.

Mary Oliver wrote in her notebook a favorite line from Archibald MacLeish. Dorothy Allison's journals contain lovely passages written by Thomas Merton and James Baldwin. The writing that ends up in my notebook defies easy description. It includes the language of surprise. Adrenaline words. Sentences that move me in ways I don't understand, that touch unfamiliar parts of me. Passages that buoy my spirit and make me bob my head in rhythm as I read along. Writing in every genre that gives fresh pleasure whenever I go back to it. Words that make me smile, shake my head, reread. Wince.

The lines and passages from other writers I copy into my notebook have one common thread: they keep me writing when my spirits falter.

Collecting the words of writers I admire can feel like chasing after them. And I'm well aware that there are many writers I'll never catch. But they write so beautifully I don't mind.

I have been inspired by Raymond Carver, not only his work but the courageous way he reclaimed his life from a history of alcoholism. Carver is most known for his short stories, but he also wrote a great deal of poetry. I admire the spirit of this poem:

Gravy
No other word will do. For that's what it was. Gravy.
Gravy, these past ten years.
Alive, sober, working, loving and
being loved by a good woman. Eleven years
ago he was told he had six months to live
at the rate he was going. And he was going
nowhere but down. So he changed his ways
somehow. He quit drinking! And the rest?
After that it was *all* gravy, every minute
of it, up to and including when he was told about,
well, some things that were breaking down and
building up inside his head. "Don't weep for me,"
he said to his friends. "I'm a lucky man.
I've had ten years longer than I or anyone
expected. Pure gravy. And don't forget it."

Passages or poems like this can be quite long, so get in the habit of being selective. Cherry-pick no more than the words you want. What ends up in my notebook is only the sweetest meat: a brief passage, a golden line, a single phrase:

It was a spring day, the sort of day that gives people hope: all soft winds and delicate smells of warm earth. Suicide weather. (from *Girl, Interrupted*, by Susanna Kaysen)

[Love] is the anesthetic Nature employs to extract babies from us. (from *Brazil*, by John Updike)

These passages inspire and instruct me. I see how Kaysen crafts her deceptive lead, beginning with a soothing description that lulls me into complacency before the shocking fragment: *suicide weather*. Updike reteaches me the importance of brevity. Say it well and move on.

Often I am struck by some unpublished writing by an author who has no fame. Marly, a third grader, wrote a poem in which she came up with a delicious line I admire very much:

The sky has the earth in its arms

And Diana Durham, a member of my poetry group, wrote a poem describing an encounter with the sea that includes this haunting line:

The cold spray air loosened a skin from me

A passage may end up in my notebooks because it models something I *don't* do, or don't do well, in my own writing. This passage about locusts is taken from James Agee's novel *A Death in the Family*:

> The noise of the locust is dry, and it seems not to be rasped or vibrated but urged from him as if through a small orifice by a breath that can never give out. Also there is never one locust but an illusion of at least a thousand. The noise of each locust is pitched in some classic locust range out of which none of them varies more than two full tones: and yet you seem to hear each locust discrete from the rest, and there is a long, slow, pulse in their noise, like the scarcely defined arch of a long and high set bridge. . . .

Reading this passage made me realize that I don't tend to do much with sound in my writing. It is remarkable the way Agee is able to sustain this evocative description, much as the locust sustains its plaintive song.

There's another kind of writing I collect not because of its searing intensity or penetrating insight but because it is flat-out fun. I love writers who don't take themselves too seriously.

(X. J. Kennedy and Tom Robbins come to mind.) Linda Pastan must have had a blast writing this poem:

Jump Cabling

When our cars	touched
When you lifted the hood	of mine
To see the intimate workings	underneath,
When we were bound	together
By a pulse of pure	energy,
When my car like the	princess
In the tale woke with a	start,

I thought why not ride the rest of the way together?

It's also interesting to find a poem or passage in which serviceable language rubs against the astonishing. Such writing is especially interesting to me because it makes visible the steps that lead to such dazzling imagery. The following poem by Robert Morgan gets its own page in my notebook because of the way he mixes the everyday with the sublime:

Honey

Only calmness will reassure
the bees to let you rob their hoard.
Any sweat of fear provokes them.
Approach with confidence, and from
the side, not shading their entrance.
And hush smoke gently from the spout
of the pot of rags, for sparks will
anger them. If you go near bees
every day they will know you.
And never jerk or turn so quick
you excite them. If weeds are trimmed
around the hive they have access
and feel free. When they taste your smoke
they fill themselves with honey and
are lazy and laden as you
lift the lid to let in daylight.

No bee full of sweetness wants to
sting. Resist greed. With the top off
you touch the fat gold frames, each cell
a hex perfect as a snowflake,
a sealed relic of sun and time
and roots of many acres fixed
in crystal-tight arrays, in rows
and lattices of sweeter latin
from scattered prose of meadow, wood.

This poem initially describes the world of beekeeping in language that is concrete and unadorned. Reading this I'm thinking, *Hey, I could probably write this, on a good day, under the right conditions.* And I'm thinking this way right up to "around the hive they have access / and feel free." At this point the poem lifts itself into a new realm; the language becomes lyrical; the final eight lines take my breath away.

I am also drawn to language that describes the physical world without resorting to sentimentality, as in this description of a she-wolf in Cormac McCarthy's novel, *The Crossing.* These unflinching words cut down to an elemental core inside me.

At this season the does were already carrying calves and as they commonly aborted long before term the ones least favored so twice she found these pale unborn still warm and gawking on the ground, milkblue and near translucent in the dawn like beings miscarried from another world. She ate even their bones where they lay blind and dying in the snow.

What poems or passages take your breath away? What words allow you to break your cocoon of silence and give you the courage to write? Keep an eye out for writing you admire and copy it into your notebook.

For me it comes down to this: *I want to surround the words I write in my notebook with the most beautiful writing I can find.* In the end I tend to choose writing not so much for its technical virtuosity but because of the way it touches my gut.

Don Murray had a daughter who died when she was twenty. Don has written many poems and essays about this, but the piece I will never forget is a poem he brought to our poetry group one evening.

Lee
Remember me not
when I was kept from you
in the waiting room, not
when I sat in the office signing
your dying, not
when I pushed you on the swing
higher than you had ever flown
and you looked back as I grew small,
certain that I would always be able to
save you.

10

A Place to Write Badly

We need our bad poems.

William Stafford

Whenever I buy a new notebook I run my hands over the empty pages and tell myself: *This notebook is going to look nice. No chicken scratchings or cross-outs this time. No more junk I'll never reread. This notebook is going to look and sound beautiful.*

For a page or two I keep this resolution. I take pains to make each letter stand up straight; I choose words that sound clear and definitive. For a few pages it does look like how I imagine a proper writer's notebook should, until some idea grabs me and sends the pen helter-skeltering across the page. I cross out one sentence, draw a heavy line beneath it, start again, scribble an arrow connecting this entry to that. Within minutes my notebook resembles all the others that preceded it.

I always forget how awkward and messy it is when you try something for the first time. When my sons Taylor and Adam took their first ski lessons the instructor greeted them by saying: "Morning, guys. You're going to fall down a lot today. But you're going to learn to ski."

For an hour and a half I witnessed their failures, lost balances, yelps of frustration, tears. I saw several spectacular falls that had me cursing myself for not bringing the camcorder. But by the end of the day they were whizzing past me on the intermediate slope. Like: *What's the big deal?*

We need to allow ourselves to fail. I have learned and re-learned this watching my kids struggle to walk, talk, read. It would be much neater if we could all somehow skip the failure stage—go directly to expert—but we can't. We need to hit the ball into the other court. We need those cooking fiascos. All our later competence is built on early wipeout and disaster.

Not many of us are brave or brazen enough to go public and let the world judge our early failed writings. That's where the notebook comes in. It gives us a private place to write badly.

In a different context Nietzche once wrote: "Much dung must be spread so that a single flower can grow." The noteboook is where I spread my manure—I lay it on thick and moist. I figure I'm fertilizing the soil from which all my future writing will flower.

It's not that I *try* to write badly in my notebook. But I know I will be doing exactly that, just like countless other writers before me. If you read the notebooks of famous writers you'll find some wonderful writing, sure enough, but you'll also find pages and pages of stuff that is surprisingly boring and tedious. In a strange sort of way I find this comforting and even inspiring.

Your ability to get the most out of your notebook depends on your ability to accept failure, tons of it. My notebook is full of failed language experiments, passages whose syntax gets all knotted up, poems that fall apart halfway through. For example:

Venus Flytrap
Let's face facts: I'm bought by
bloodthirsty fifth-grade boys
eager to impress their friends
or gross out some girl
they secretly love.

My nickname? Plant Dracula.
They consider me a monster,
some carnivorous freak

but here's the truth: I am
monstrously misunderstood.

Easy to be like other flowers,
flashing around gaudy colors
to attract bees. I aim to attract
pesky flies and eliminate them
without a trace. Not bad, eh?

I sort of like the beginning of this poem but it starts to disinte-
grate in the second stanza. And the ending truly reeks. Maybe
later on I'll be able to salvage part of this but for now I'm happy
to leave the mess and move on.

Another time I wrote this fictitious description of a woman
sitting alone in a house at night:

The moonlight on the porcelain snow cast a flat unearthly lumi-
nescence into the house, a voidal light that further whitened
her exsanguine complexion and made her eyes glow even
darker—like diamonds infuriated at having ever been cut from
stone—smouldering where she sat in the corner.

How's that for purple prose? This passage comes from my early
look-Ma-I'm-writing period, when I seemed determined to include as many highfalutin words (voidal light?) as possible in
everything I wrote. But bad as it is, a passage like this has its
purpose. I'm pushing my vocabulary, taking chances, trying
stuff. I'm practicing the craft.

Near the end of *The Pharoah's War,* by Tobias Wolff, the narrator describes what it's like to write a first novel. He could just
as easily be describing a writer's notebook:

I knew it wasn't very good, but I also knew that it was the best I
could do just then and that I had to keep doing it if I ever
wanted to get any better. These words would never be read by
anyone, I understood, but even in sinking out of sight they
made the ground more solid under my hope to write well.

11

Compost and Transformation

Notebooks also contain the raw material from which new works of art are made. They precede selection and are like experience itself—a lively disorder of events and impressions whose very juxtaposition can be refreshing.

Frank McShane

My compost heap isn't much to look at: six posts set in a circle and strung with heavy-gauge chicken wire, the structure five feet in diameter and five feet high. Composting is not very complicated. Some people get pretty serious about it—there are books to explain everything you ever wanted to know about the chemistry of decomposing vegetable matter—but it's not rocket science. Basically all I do is throw in my grass clippings plus any leftover vegetable matter and wait for Mother Nature to work her magic and turn it back into dirt.

You can tell if the compost is "cooking" by the pungent smell of rotting vegetables. Reach your hand into an active compost and you'll be amazed: it's hot. Some people even buy special thermometers to measure exactly how hot. That heat gets generated from the bacterial action taking place as the rotting vegetable matter breaks down into dark nutritious soil.

After the autumn harvest a Great Exchange takes place between my vegetable garden and the compost heap. I uproot my leftover vegetable plants in the garden and throw them into the compost heap. At the same time I dig out the thick, rich composted dirt, haul it over to the garden, and work it into the soil for next year's crop.

The notebook as compost heap? Why not? While it may not be the perfect metaphor, it does suggest several crucial aspects of the notebook:

- *Transformation*. Like a compost heap, a writer's notebook is all about change, commonplace ingredients simmering in a slow hot stew until they get tranformed into something new and valuable.
- *Fertility*. Nature's most extravagant spending sprees are connected to the fertility cycle: millions of lobster eggs, legions of sperm sprinting toward the egg, zillions of bacterial microbes in the compost heap. Compost heaps and notebooks share a fertility that is ongoing and mysterious.
- *Randomness*. Like the compost heap, a writer's notebook typically does not have separate compartments for particular kinds of entries. You just throw stuff in, whatever you've got.
- *Wait time*. The compost heap requires the patience to wait about a year for today's uneaten salad to transform itself into tomorrow's high-class soil. The writer's notebook often requires something similar. Pause. Hold. Wait.

One morning a few years ago I walked into a fifth-grade classroom in Sea Cliff, New York. Around the perimeter of the classroom I noticed about two dozen small skeletons, each one glued to its own piece of construction paper. Snake skeletons? Small rodents? An involuntary spasm shuddered up my spine.

"What are they?" I asked a boy.

"Oh those," he said in a bored voice. "We've been dissecting owl pellets."

"What's an owl pellet?" I asked. The boy just stared at me.

"You really don't know?" he asked. When I admitted that I

did not, he showed me a jar with a small brownish sack inside about three inches high.

"See, owls are carnivorous," he explained. "They eat live animals like snakes and mice, but they can't digest all the hair and bones so they cough up these owl pellets. You can find the pellets in barns or under trees. Then when you dissect them you can figure out what the owl had for dinner last night."

I stood staring at the owl pellet. It fascinated me, so dark and concentrated. So *symbolic*. I thought about it on and off throughout the day, and that night I jotted a brief entry in my writer's notebook:

> I'm in a class in Sea Cliff, New York, fifth grade, the kids have these skeletons of tiny animals pasted onto cardboard. Small rodents, mice, birds. A boy explained that owls can't digest all of the animals they eat so they spit up a little pouch that has hair/bones/skin etc. of the eaten animal. Owl pellets! Bag of bones! A doggie bag from hell! Where have *I* been? Almost forty years old—how come I never heard of them???

Not everything strikes my imagination but for some reason this owl pellet did. It had the heft and feel of a genuine trigger I would explore further on another day. But now that I had written the entry I moved onto something else.

Ten months later I was hard at work on a book of poems about love. I was scouring the pages of my notebook, hot for any possible ideas, when I stumbled onto the entry about the owl pellets. Owl pellets seemed an unlikely idea for a love poem, which, of course, was exactly what made it so appealing. In this case the poem came quickly. I strongly doubt the raw entry would ever have turned into a finished poem without the months it spent composting in my notebook.

Owl Pellets
In biology class
you sit close to me,
knee touching mine,

your sweet smell
almost drowning out
the formaldehyde stink
which crinkles up your nose
while I dissect
our fetal pig.

Now we dissect owl pellets,
small bags of skin and bones,
what the owl ate
but couldn't digest
and coughed back up.

You sit with Jon Fox,
laugh at his dumb jokes,
let your head fall
onto his bony shoulder
while I try to piece together
the tiny bones
of a baby snake.

Certain things
are almost
impossible
to swallow.

12

Divining Rod: Summoning the Deep Water

I have just reread my year's diaries and am much struck by the rapid haphazard gallop at which it swings along. . . . Still if it were not written rather faster than the fastest type-writing, if I stopped and took thought, it would never be written at all; and the advantage of the method is that it sweeps up accidentally several stray matters which I should exclude if I hesitated, but which are the diamonds of the dustheap.

Virginia Woolf

Some writers claim they never revisit their notebooks. But most of us go back incessantly, rummaging, rereading, looking for—what? For me, I usually don't know what I'm looking for until I find it. And then: aha!

Too often I have only vague feelings and sort-of ideas when I begin to write. I sit at my desk with a sinking feeling because I know that such generalities spell death to a piece of writing. This is where my notebook comes in handy. Rereading it is like rolling up my sleeves and immersing my arms up to the elbows in hot particulars. In all the possibilities that exist in words. More often than not, this gets me back on track.

I reread my notebooks in several different ways:

- At times I reread deliberately, conscious that I'm looking for material to write about.

- I may reread in a brisk, random way, skimming without any precise purpose, my eyes chancing on this line or that image. This kind of rereading often gets me in the mood to write.
- If I'm about to begin a piece of writing, I am often looking for the appropriate voice. Rereading several notebook entries written in different voices can help me settle on the voice I want.
- Sometimes I'm looking only for material about a particular theme—entries pertaining to love, for instance, or references to my son Robert. With this kind of rereading I try to be blind to all the other kinds of entries.

Overall I tend to reread haphazardly; you may be more systematic. Either way, reread until you find a line or phrase or idea that intrigues you enough to pursue further. Then start writing on a fresh piece of paper or try a draft in your notebook. The notebook may not be the place where you bring the rough idea to polished completion (at some point you may want to move to a legal pad or a computer monitor) but it gives you a place to at least begin shaping selected material.

While rereading a notebook I stumbled onto the entry mentioned in Chapter 5, a fragment I overheard on the radio: "In our lifetime we may see the end of the shellfish industry." I felt the mingled tugs of sadness and anger and vivid memory. I recalled a first unforgettable experience as a boy eating a steamer clam hot off the grill in Sofie Pratt's backyard in Marshfield, Massachusetts. I flashed on all the lonely afternoons I spent digging littleneck clams on Long Island's Great South Bay. I remembered being just out of college with my whole life before me and eating oysters by the dozen, a dime apiece, at a restaurant in New Orleans. Envisioning a future in which shellfish were extinct, I started to write a poem about it. The finished work is quite long, but here's the beginning:

Aftertaste
Imagine, my love: conch, quahog,
scallop and scungilli all extinct.
Of course we'll be older then
in looser more comfortable skin
lying in bed and allowing ourselves
what we would never permit now,
an afternoon glass of burgundy.

As I reread I often find myself drawn to entries that reflect tension or paradox—opposing forces that are unresolved. While turning the pages of a notebook recently I came across a number of these entries:

This Christmas everyone's healthy. The whole house is decorated. So why all this tension in the family? Where's it coming from?

Mom, peaceful woman, a dove if there ever was one, is fascinated with World War II movies. She's seen them all.

Man at the garden store: "The rose is like any other bush—the harder you prune it the better it grows."

Paul took me to Thetford to meet Jake, a gray-haired farmer. Jake made a divining rod out of a cut green bough, and showed me how to use it. It worked! Felt a hard downward pull when I took a step.

Almost twenty years passed before I returned to that entry about the divining rod. Reading it again brought back the confusion of the initial experience. I did not (and still tend not to) believe in such things; still, my own hands felt an undeniable downward pull that seemed to be coming from the ground. The more I thought about this incident the more curious I became. I began to try out a poem, and after a dozen drafts, this is what I had:

The Divining Rod
A green bough cut into a rough V
held taut between my thumbs
suspended above the ground.
I walked. Nothing. Then:

a gentle tugging on my hands
like an invisible fish striking,
now a sustained downward pull
as if the earth itself
wanted me back.

I was twenty-two years old
and everything amazed me:
the integers of a woman's spine,
the splendor of winter stars
that had long since burned out,
a strange woman I met at a party
who followed me into the bathroom
and peed calmly while explaining
her theory on Italian filmmaking.

At night there is a particular
voice of yours that pulls me down
and conjures up that insistent tug
of water or rock or simple earth.
I am older now, I tell myself
such things are not possible.
How easily do I betray these
hands that surely felt it,
that feel it now.

You won't always hit paydirt when you go back and reread
your notebook. I once saw a moth in a corner of our garage resting a few inches beneath the web of a fat spider. This seemed
like a strange place for an insect to alight so I came closer to in-
vestigate. When I touched the moth I saw that it was dead,
feather-light, its insides sucked dry by the spider. When I revisit
the triggers in my notebooks I often discover that the initial
idea that had seemed so ripe and promising turns out to be as
dry and false as an empty insect husk.

Don't despair when that happens. You may come back to it
in another year or two. But most likely it's a dud. (My notebook

is filled with them.) As you reread you'll find plenty of ideas that fall short and fail to trigger anything more than boredom. Finding an idea that intrigues you enough to pursue it is more the exception than the rule.

There are other reasons an idea may not immediately inspire you to further writing. As I reread my notebook I often come upon emotionally charged entries I'm still not ready to write about. Ten months later, the entry about my mother's stopped heart during surgery still seems too raw. My instinct is not to write about an idea like this. Yet.

When you reread your notebook you may encounter a particular passage more than once. Not the exact same passage, but similar material with a similar urge behind it. Don't be surprised. Pay close attention to these recurring themes because they tell you where your true interests lie as a writer. Those obsessions often spark your best writing.

Certain subjects show up again and again in my notebooks: water, light, love, babies, crystals, mushrooms, fire, spiders, clams. For me, these objects hold a kind of magic. Each time I reread another entry on one of these subjects I get a stronger sense of the magic. While glancing through my notebook I rediscovered this entry, mentioned earlier:

> Found a rusty cull rack in the pile of junk Mom was throwing out.
> Reminded me of digging clams with Bob. I decided to keep it.

This entry connects two recurring themes in my notebooks: clam digging and the death of my brother Bob. In this case I tried to "follow the golden thread," as William Stafford suggested, and see what would happen. Beginning to write opened a flood of associated memories connected to the cull rack. I wrote eight or ten drafts and ended up with this:

The Cull Rack
At the driveway's end
broken screens, worn-out rakes,
croquet set missing every mallet

66

except one, and an old cull rack
from my clam-digging days.

I try to pull out the rack
but it catches on something
before it finally comes free:
eight bars, well rusted,
set in a rickety frame.

My middle brother Bob
clammed along side me,
a glorious stupor of sweat,
sun, bay muck and horseflies.
We dumped what we caught—
chowders, cherries, littlenecks—
into the shallow cull rack
and shook vigorously
so the tasty seedlings
could fall through the bars
for some later harvest.

We averaged maybe a bushel
to a bushel and a half
bought at the dock by serious men
standing by huge empty trucks
who weighed our clams
                on their scales
and paid us each day in cash
rounded off to the nearest
five dollars.

I still think of him
as a kid who should have
slipped through
the random harvest of
that high school car wreck
to grow old, or old enough
for a car, some memorable sex,

maybe a child of his own,
old enough for his lean belly
to go soft and loose
like the rest of us

though this cull rack
isn't in bad shape at all
when you really look at it:
a few nails and some steel wool
will make it almost
good as new.

13

Escaping from the Monkey Trap

The notebook is experimental writing in the best sense. Any-thing can be tried because nothing is at stake. No one is watch-ing; there is no script, as there is in rehearsal, to obey.

Howard Junker

When I began to write I took the most natural subject around: my oversized family. Being the oldest of nine chil-dren. The death of my brother. My matriarchical grand-mother. The bluff and bluster of my Irish uncles. Growing up Catholic in the sixties and early seventies when our house got invaded by hip guitar-playing priests. Moving from Marshfield, Massachusetts, to Winnetka, Illinois, and the sudden shock of rubbing my middle-class shoulders with the rich and beautiful.

I grew up swimming in stories. When I started to write I be-gan dutifully retelling those tales. This had certain advan-tages—unlike some writers I knew, I never ran out of material. But writing those family stories turned out to be more compli-cated than I had imagined.

Take, for instance, the summer a boy from the Chicago housing projects spent two weeks at our house through the Fresh Air program. The story of Willie Poole got told and re-told so many times in my family it took on the quality of an heirloom. Years later, when I began writing about Willie, I wondered: *Whose experience do I tell? mine? the family's? Willie's? As the "writer in the family" didn't I have a responsibility to be cool and objective, to preserve the family lore? Who was I to alter a family heirloom?*

And what about the tension between the official version of a story and my own perceptions? For example, the official family version said that my brother's death in 1974 was a tragedy, pure and simple. But that version leaves out the troublesome fact that these high school seniors jumped into a car after they'd all been drinking.

In certain parts of Africa there is a particular kind of trap traditionally used to capture monkeys. The trap is a hollow coconut half-filled with rice, with a hole just big enough for one of the monkey's hands to fit through. The monkey reaches in and grabs a fistful of rice. But when he tries to escape he discovers that now his rice-filled fist will not slide back out of the trap. The monkey stands there, helplessly pulling, stuck, until he gets captured. It never occurs to the monkey to drop the rice.

That monkey was me as a young writer. Fists crammed full of the precious rice of my life. Unable to let go of even a single grain. So fixated on truth and accuracy I wouldn't allow myself to shape any of the stories that were my inheritance as a writer. I was stuck. I couldn't grow, I couldn't move forward.

We can write right up to the edge of what novelist Tim O'Brien calls the "happening truth" of an event. But that's not enough. It's in the next step—when we step off into the unknown and try to craft the "story truth"—that the real writing begins.

I am learning to let go of all that rice. I've had to learn how to drop it, not all of it, but enough so I can slide my hand out of the trap and move on. This hasn't been easy, but with the help of several wonderful writing mentors I have slowly learned to leave behind some of the "truth" in my stories, to alter and embellish them, combine them, play with them. This kind of reshaping often takes place in my notebook, where I give myself generous permission to take chances and experiment, even if it means falling on my face.

Writers often use their notebook as a place to play. Novelist Dorothy Allison describes her journal as a "playground." And writer Sherman Alexie says:

> [In my notebook] I like to play with already-printed material: questionnaires, greeting cards, calendars, other people's letters. Newspaper articles, *TV Guide*, magazines, and such. I always try to surprise myself with these, look at language in new ways. All these things also serve as springboards for real poems and stories.

In this chapter I want to look at a half-dozen ways I use my notebook to play with ideas.

The What If? *Game*

Here are the facts: Michael's mother teaches sixth grade. Michael is also in sixth grade, same school, different teacher. One day his mom brought something special home from school: a bag of eyeballs, actual pigs' eyes. They had just arrived for the science unit. Michael was enthralled by the eyeballs and their eerie resemblance to human eyes. He invited three friends over so they could take a close look. Melanie, his high school sister, said they were the "grossest things" she'd ever seen.

This little story intrigued me. I wrote about it in my notebook and, later, gave my imagination free rein to play the *what if?* game. What if instead of his mother Michael's real teacher gave him a half-dozen pigs' eyes to take home for the night? What if Michael had a devilish streak in him? What if Michael wanted to get back at his sister for some reason? Could he somehow use the pigs' eyes to freak her out—maybe put them in her purse or soap dish?

I use a hybrid of this idea in a novel, *Spider Boy*. The narrator, Bobby, and his big sister, Breezy, are at each other's throats during most of the book. Bobby despises Breezy's new boyfriend, Luke. Bobby secretly brings home six pigs' eyes he got from a friendly science teacher the same day Luke comes over for dinner. While setting the table Bobby has a stroke of inspiration: he puts the eyes in the olive bowl, staring straight up, buried under one layer of olives. The ensuing dinner is memorable. This scene was great fun to write—it's the kind of practical joke I would have never dared to play when I was a kid.

Cross-Pollination

A friend of mine had just graduated from college and was looking for a job. We spent the weekend together revising his résumé and looking at want ads.

On Monday I sat down with my notebook. I had been playing around with a collection of flower poems and wanted to include a poem about the wildflowers that always manage to sneak into the gardens we plant. I closed my eyes to picture a wildflower, but all I saw were hundreds of want ads. Aha! An offbeat way to approach the wildflower poem.

Wildflowers

Help wanted: sturdy individuals
interested in grass-roots work
at a number of rugged locations
(cliffs, desert, some tundra).
Good benefits. Must be strong
and adaptable, self-starter,
persistent, willing to relocate,
with no fear of high places
and no known allergies
to bees.

This reveals the kind of notebook play I do all the time— connecting two disparate forms or ideas and seeing what might result. Try it. A story written as a series of memos. A cookbook written by an ant. A letter from your chapped winter hands. These kinds of hybrids sometimes pull your writing in a new direction that leads to a vein of rich and unexpected ore.

Collecting

I was reading *Bitter Bananas*, a picture book by Isaac Olaleye, to my two-year-old. Halfway through we came upon the word *twilight*.

"What's twilight?" Joseph wanted to know.

"Well, it's not light but it's not really dark," I explained. "It's kind of an in between time of day."

For the moment that satisfied Joseph. But the next time we read that book and came upon that word he asked again: "What's twilight?" I could tell he was intrigued, so I explained again, adding more details.

One day I wrote a line in my notebook: "Morning twilight erases the blackboard of stars." A few months later I reread that line. There was something pleasing to my ear about that sentence—its simple, clear ring. I wrote several more lines related to twilight. Over the next three weeks I filled six notebook pages with lines, ideas, and associations related to dawn and dusk. In the following notebook entries you can see the idea developing:

> Morning twilight seeps in before the sun is up. A few stars or bright planets remain, unstolen jewels in the changing sky.
>
> Summer twilight trips on the streetlights, hisses on the sprinklers, flushes out the mosquitoes and bats to eat them.
>
> Something about fireflies
>
> Winter twilight puts a lovely sheen of china blue onto the white snow.
>
> Dawn and dusk—the crack between the worlds of darkness and light. Or dawn as a seed that grows into full daylight.

Maybe a pattern book—Morning Twilight, Night Twilight? Dawn and Dusk? Twilight, Twice?

I often use my notebook to collect ideas about a subject that interests me. I feel powerful when I do this, even though I know I may only use a fraction of what I collect or might abandon the idea entirely. In this case I liked the writing enough to want to collect more. Maybe I was onto something. I took the next step and began working on a picture book manuscript, *Twilight Comes Twice*.

When you find a writing idea that piques your interest you can use your notebook to collect any facts, myths, feelings, lines, ideas, questions, dreams, and references connected to it. Try to be generous; don't censor or judge too critically when you play with an idea like this. Peter Elbow has said that a skilled writing teacher must be both a "good host and a good bouncer." Well said! The same is true for a skilled writer. Later you can scrutinize your finished text all you like, but while collecting ideas you want to be the quintessential good host, smiling, affirming. Invite in all your ideas, even the ones that arrive in dyed hair and outlandish clothes, the ones that don't really seem to belong.

Layering

On page 145 of my notebook I come upon this entry:

Playing BORNED w/Taylor and Adam

Like many of my entries this one works as verbal shorthand, inscrutable to anybody else but me. I know what it means; in fact, rereading it warms a part of me. Rereading it I'm drawn to try a draft:

At first, JoAnn's two boys and I didn't know each other too well. I tried to make them comfortable with me. We played school, and Rough, but their favorite game was called Borned.

I'd lay down on the floor on one side. My head rested on my right hand so a triangle was formed between my head and bent

74

arm. Taylor and Adam scurried behind me and started pushing through this triangular hole. First Taylor came through, then Adam. I'd tend to them like newborn babies, cradling them, cooing at them, squeezing their cheeks.

"It's wonderful," JoAnn's mother said, watching us. "It's like the boys are getting born into a brand-new family."

In my notebook I may do four or five drafts of the same piece. Don Murray calls this process *layering*, going over the same material, digging deeper, looking for surprises. It may seem odd to draft on blank notebook pages, but that's what I do and I find the process invaluable. It helps me nail down many variables— voice, pacing, shape, crucial details.

While layering this piece I decided not to change the ending. But I wanted to slow down the beginning of the piece and present a clearer picture of Taylor and Adam. In the next draft I added a number of details describing the characters so that it now takes much longer to get to the first mention of playing Borned.

> When I got married to JoAnn her two boys and I didn't know each other terribly well. Taylor was six, a tall skinny boy who loved to collect, sort, and race Matchbox™ cars. I thought he looked spookily like his mother. Adam was three: an exuberant kid who never met a food he didn't like. He was just out of diapers but already built strong and stocky as a miniature linebacker.
>
> I played with Taylor and Adam whenever I had the chance. We played hide-'n'-go-seek, and Rough, and school, standing in the kitchen with hands on our hearts and pledging allegiance to an imaginary flag on the wall. But their favorite game by far was called Borned.

Exercises

Many writers swear by writing exercises—bully for them. I'll admit it: I've got a bad attitude when it comes to writing exercises, but I can't help it. To me the writing exercise is a by-product of the fifty-minute English class: the prompt written on the board, the quick-write, hand it in, oops, there's the bell. Just take these vitamins and do these easy exercises and I guarantee that within four weeks your stomach will be rippled like a washboard! Do these simple exercises and within a matter of weeks you'll be a real writer!

Yeah, sure.

Regular, sustained writing—that's the only way to master this difficult craft. Writing exercises: who needs them?

I do, sometimes.

At a conference two young high school teachers suggested playing mood music to encourage students to write. *Let's try it now*, one of them said. I silently rolled my eyes as they switched on a portable stereo. Then the music started. At first I resisted but within moments I could feel those notes enter and calm me from the inside out. I wrote:

Coltrane
You gave me the depths
the sweet inside scoop
speakeasy of my soul
music I had never known
soft sultry as rustled silk
bass notes thum-thumping
each of my trembling ribs
that never seemed like
a prison to my heart
when I lay beside you

This poem exists solely because that exercise, that music, brought it to life.

There are books for writers crammed with suggested exercises, though it isn't hard to devise your own exercises to stretch yourself as a writer. Challenge yourself to write what's most difficult for you. Describe that man's face on the plane. The flight attendant's canned smile. The unsavory waiter at the restaurant (and your suspicion that a drop of sweat from his face fell into your veal piccata). The moment when conscious thought dissolves into sleep. Push yourself. Represent as accurately as possible the dialogue between your tight-lipped husband and silent teenaged son. Describe your best friend's most annoying gesture.

You can also stretch yourself by trying to imitate your favorite author. Is there something he or she does you'd like to try yourself? Talking directly to the reader? Inserting a parenthesis (or a parenthesis within a parenthesis)? Fragments? Perhaps you have always wanted to try your hand at stream-of-consciousness writing you know the kind of ramshackle prose that lacks any punctuation sentences that seem two maybe three sentences all rolled into one that can be really tricky to read though it's uncanny how accurately this kind of writing reflects the jumble of the thinking mind. . . . Try it out.

Invention

Raymond Carver's short story "Cathedral" involves a husband, his wife, and a blind man the wife once met on a train. The blind man comes to visit, and when the wife goes to bed, he and the husband stay up late together. The blind man is curious to learn that the husband is watching a show about cathedrals. To help him imagine a cathedral, the blind man asks the husband to guide his hand in drawing one on paper. The story turns on the moment when the blind man instructs the husband to close his eyes as he draws. To let go.

A notebook is a place to do exactly that. To let go of the rice. To let go of reporting literal events and invent what comes into your head—plots, conflicts, ideas, philosophies, characters, dialogues.

Invent the faces of characters. Autumn milkweed pods as defective pillows, the stuffing coming out. Wild violets as small purple secrets whispered all over the lawn. Come up with your own lines and triggers.

Make up conversations between yourself and an old lover or deceased relative. Take a real conversation and alter it. Invent conversations between imaginary characters. Indulge your "staircase wit"—the scathing retort you should have given that time your boss or lover cut you to the quick.

> I was driving with Bill when two women dash in front of the car. One of them flips him the bird.
>
> "Excuse me!" He motions her over to the car.
>
> "You gotta problem?" she snaps.
>
> "Here," Bill says, scribbling something on a card and handing it to her. "You seem like a nice enough person, so later I know you're going to want to apologize for being so rude to me. Here's my number."
>
> She takes the card and just stares at him.
>
> "You think I'm gonna *call* you?" She throws Bill's card at us as he drives away.

This dialogue is a complete fabrication. One day I heard these voices in my head, jabbering at each other; my notebook gave me a place to write down their talk. This may be the start of a longer piece of writing or it may be nothing more than a fragment. It was fun to write, so who cares?

14

The Set Piece: Something Small and Beautiful

In his or her journals, the writer is unprofessional, unbuttoned, unguarded. A writer uses a journal to try out the new step in front of the mirror. He or she can abandon constraints of narrative form and allow the luxury of verbal spontaneity. In journals, therefore, we often find delightful small set pieces: descriptions for their own sake, character sketches, bits of philosophy, heartfelt cries that take on a particular brightness precisely because they aren't embedded in a larger narrative.

Mary Gordon

Go to any playground and you'll see kids practicing moves. Over there that kid in the Knicks T-shirt is trying hard to balance a spinning basketball on his forefinger. On the soccer field a girl is juggling a soccer ball, seeing how many times she can hit it with her feet and knees before it hits the ground.

What's going on?

Moves like these aren't very practical. It's hard to imagine how balancing a spinning basketball or juggling a soccer ball would ever come in handy during an actual game. But they do demonstrate certain intangibles that are important to becoming a skilled player: balance, confidence, a feel for the ball. These intangibles signal membership in the club, a way for the player to announce first to him- or herself and then to the world: *I've got a little game. I can play. I belong in this league.*

My notebook is the place where I try out moves. I take an idea or technique and play with it for a stretch, seeing how long I can keep it going.

> I like towns with two-word names—New York, West Islip, Ann Arbor, Chapel Hill, Murder Creek. There's a freedom of space in two-word towns—a distance between the Chapel and the Hill, Ann and the Arbor, Murder and the Creek, that makes breathing easier. I get nervous in one word-towns. I get claustrophobic.

I dug this piece out of a notebook I kept during my late twenties. It's not profound writing that tries to touch on any immortal truth. Rather, it's reaching for ironic humor, wit. And much as it is fashionable to disown one's pathetic early writing attempts, I think this one works pretty well. I can sense the fun behind the writing, as well as the more serious long-term purpose: learning to juggle the words of my craft. Getting my balance. Finding my voice. Gaining confidence. Trying to prove to myself that I am good enough to play in this league.

The audience for this set piece was nobody but me. I fashioned it for my eyes, my practice, my pleasure. And I believe this is true for most writers. Occasionally a piece like this is a rehearsal for publishable writing, but more often it gets written for the sheer pleasure (or challenge) of the prose itself, with little worldly ambition beyond that.

The set piece is a genre specific to the writer's notebook. It can range in length from a few sentences to a few paragraphs, perhaps longer. It differs from a typical entry by its wholeness and polish. Like a poem or short story, the set piece has a distinct beginning, middle, and end. Usually it can stand on its own, separate and unattached to larger work. It is an informal genre—there are no set rules to the set piece.

The urge to craft a set piece begins with the desire to create something small and beautiful. John Cheever's journals are peppered with set pieces, so much so that at one point he complains about his tendency to write too many of them. Some of these pieces explore characters he has observed and speculated about. Others describe places, settings imbued with that famous Cheeverian light. Still others describe a particular state of mind:

> The house was dark, of course. The snow went on falling. The last of the cigarette butts was gone, the gin bottle was empty, even the aspirin supply was exhausted. He went upstairs to the medicine cabinet. The plastic vial that used to contain Miltown still held a few grains, and by wetting his finger he picked these up and ate them. They made no difference. At least we're alive, he kept saying, at least we're alive, but without alcohol, aspirin, barbituates, coffee, and tobacco it seemed to be a living death. At least I can do something, he thought, at least I can distract myself, at least I can take a walk; but when he went to the door he saw wolves on the lawn.

This set piece is not wholly fictitious; Cheever himself admitted that he struggled with various addictions during his life. Working from this autobiographical seed Cheever carefully crafts this passage with all the tools available—authentic tone, chilling detail, frame-by-frame motion, repetition, voice. Interesting that he chooses to write about this character through the third person "he" instead of the "I." The final image of the wolves brings this piece to a definite and disturbing end.

If a novel is a marathon, the set piece is a sprint. Reading the set pieces from various authors' notebooks you can sense their pleasure in writing a brief stretch of prose without having the additional pressure of having to integrate it into a novel or short story. The notebooks of Dorianne Laux contain several set pieces that portray a vision of the world, a vision grounded in memorable particularity.

I have always loved the world, in spite of itself, the chancreous volcanos, the lurid eye of the Iguana, the lure of black water. I guess because it gives back what it takes, manure to flower, dead wood to mushroom, water to rain. Even when the worst was upon me, the father's belly large with his children's souls, even as the light was sucked from my mouth, my eyes darkening, even then, I watched the fly climb the wall, iridescent, winged, a holy image to carry with me until I woke.

Usually I wait for something to inspire a set piece of writing. But I sometimes take a more active role and give myself a specific writing task I sense might stretch me.

In early autumn I went with my family to a restaurant at York Beach in Maine. When we arrived the restaurant had not yet opened, so we took the kids across the street to the beach. The beach was beautiful and cold and strangely moving at low tide. *Write about this*, I told myself; the next day I did.

Went to Mimmo's yesterday. The restaurant wasn't open yet so we wandered across the street to kill time. Clear, sunny, cold on the beach. It was low tide with a strong onshore wind and lots of long shadows and everything illuminated by pure slanting late afternoon light. As if we were all exactly halfway between two worlds: day and night, land and sea, earth and sky. The sand dark with dry whiter sand blowing over it. The dry sand made ghostly ribbons, white snakes; Joseph and Robert squealed chasing them down to the water's edge. I was ravenous. My nose was twitching, torn between the smell of the sea and the aroma wafting from the restaurant, pungent rivers of butter and garlic snaking invisibly through the air.

Writing like this feels as satisfying as being alone and hitting a tennis ball against a smooth wall, trying to hit it flat and low and hard: whap! whap! whap! whap! I'm trying out a new move: describing a particular place at a specific time of day. I give myself lots of room to play even as I try, finally, to bring the piece to some small resolution, to polish it, to produce an effect for an imagined reader.

You can use your notebook to try out set pieces. If you're looking for a subject, you might reread your notebook and see whether a line or image jumps out at you. Or use what is close at hand. Is there a character around town you have watched and wondered about? Is there a particular gesture your father makes, a ritual he plays out at the end of your family gatherings? Is there a special Sunday night breed of despair you feel, exhausted by the weekend, not yet ready to face Monday morning? It usually takes me a few drafts until the set piece sounds the way I want; set pieces are usually short enough that I can try two or three versions on a double notebook page.

Getting in the habit of crafting and polishing set pieces in your notebook can help you acquire the moves and bounce and stride of a writer. The set piece may be foremost an act of playfulness and pleasure, but when skillfully done it has an undeniable value of its own.

> When I am dead, make of my skin a sounding board. Drum out hope where there was none before. Make a timpani of my bones and despair. Go past shame and remember me as I truly was, child of a family not meant to survive who lived anyway. Remember me, the one who loved well the women in her life.
>
> Dorothy Allison

15

Writing About Writing

Every poem is an infant labored into birth and I am drenched with sweating effort, tired from the pain and hurt of being a man, in the poem I transform myself into a woman.

Jimmy Santiago Baca

Writing is hard. It's easy to develop new and vigorous hybrids of self-loathing as the rejection notices arrive in the mail and your best friend's novel gets a rave in the *New York Times*.

If you are serious about writing, you want to last over the long haul. And if you hope to last, it is crucial to learn how to be gentle with yourself. To forgive yourself completely, as William Stafford said. To be patient when the writing doesn't flow strong and sweet. To reward yourself in little ways—a walk through the woods, chunk of dark chocolate, juicy clementine, hot bath—when you have done a decent writing stint or, equally important, cleared away the minutiae that will allow you to write.

Open a bottle of wine and you fill everyone else's glass before your own. At supper you serve the children before you serve yourself, right? Fine. But in your notebook you can serve yourself first.

First person. The notebook is the place to take care of the writer inside you. To keep the writing flame lit amid the winds of indifference. This is important because nobody else will care about your writing as much as you.

How do you keep that flame alive? By writing every day. By

telling your side of the story, uninterrupted. Your feelings, long-ings, minute observations. By recording the witty thing you said (even if only in your head) at your son's graduation. By having one place in your life where you don't have to lie to yourself.

I know that writing is hard so I do whatever I can to make it easier. In my notebook I tape in friendly letters from editors—even rejection notices that have encouraging handwritten notes.

And, like other writers, I include in my notebook thoughts about writing. I collect a hodgepodge of rantings and ravings, inspirational sayings, other writer's thoughts, plus my own rumi-nations on the subject. These entries vary widely but they have certain things in common. They all speak *from the inside* about the writer's craft. They acknowledge that writing is exasperat-ing, impossible. And in some indefinable way these words give me hope, they give me courage, they keep me writing. Here is a selection of other writers' insights about the craft:

> The world is full of poets with languid wrenches who don't bother to take the last six turns on their bolts.
>
> X. J. Kennedy

> I like poems in fragments, things with rough and sharp edges that sometimes cut unexpectedly, that cannot be handled too easily and always with safety. One piece of broken quartz can shave an ax handle, same as an expensive plane. Lines are pieces of the shattered original diamond.
>
> Robert Morgan

> Sincere love poems aren't good. Good love poems aren't sincere.
>
> Vern Rutsala

> "Sometimes," said Whitey Ford, the great Yankee curveballer, "you need to put one right down the middle." He was speaking of surprises. I always thought that poets, especially abstruse po-ets, could profit by his remark.
>
> Stephen Dunn

In writing you work toward a result you won't see for years, and can't be sure you'll ever see. It takes stamina and self-mastery and faith. It demands those things of you, then gives them back with a little extra, a surprise to keep you coming. It toughens you and clears your head.

Tobias Wolff

Writing a novel is like driving a car at night. You can see only as far as your headlights, but you can make the whole trip that way.

E. L. Doctorow

The first draft is the down draft—you just get it down. The second draft is the up draft—you fix it up. The third draft is the dental draft, when you check every tooth, to see if it's loose or cramped or decayed, or even, God help us, healthy.

Ann Lamott

About poems that don't work—who wants to see a bird almost fly?

Mary Oliver

People who say the novel is dead are wrong. The novel is not dead. The novel is going to be at your funeral.

Richard Price

16

Writing at the Border: Dangerous Words

Cracking open the inner world again, writing even a couple of pages, threw me back into depression, not made easier by the weather, two gloomy days of darkness and rain. I was attacked by a storm of tears, those tears that appear to be related to frustration, to buried anger, and come upon me without warning. I woke yesterday so depressed that I did not get up till after eight.

May Sarton

One morning I was sitting in a coffee shop with a close friend. He had just gone through a serious bout with depression. After several months he was finally coming out of it.

"You know, about a month ago I had this strange realization," he said. "I said to myself: *I'll have to kill myself before I kill myself.*"

I sat up straight and looked at him.

"What do you mean?"

"Well, I realized I'd have to kill *the idea of myself* before I actually carried out the act," he replied.

This is the chapter about writing from the heart. If that's too touchy-feely for you, go on ahead, I'll catch up.

Still with me? Good: I think this is important. I believe that you can find energy as a writer by approaching borders—the edge of language, the limbus of your history, the outermost limit of your fears. The most difficult subjects. Your notebook gives you a way to move closer to that border, or even cross it. Writing at the border has its therapeutic benefits, no doubt, but it can also spark your deepest, truest writing.

Hemingway talked about sitting down and writing one true sentence. But it's not always easy to admit the truth, let alone write it. A few years ago our family went on vacation with another family; we rented a small house in Denmark. Our friends had a two-year-old child; one night the little boy got an earache that kept everyone up all night. At one point the husband, exhausted to the point of despair, muttered: "I hate my job, I hate my family, I hate my life."

Whoa. I was shocked to hear this from a man I knew genuinely loves his family. But for that moment it must have been true.

That's the kind of notebook truth I'm after but it isn't easy to get. From early childhood we are socialized to be so damned polite. This training produces grownups who rarely forget to say thank you or keep our mouths closed while chewing food, but who find it almost impossible to be totally candid, even when we're writing for our own eyes only.

I'm not immune to this problem. Rereading my notebooks I come upon page after page of writing that is superficial, worthless, dishonest. Even when describing a painful family situation, I tend to "make nice" and write in a cheerful or impartial voice instead of banging on the table and screaming like I want to. These are the places where I fail myself: the real stuff of my life never gets written down.

There are several possible explanations for why we so often pull punches when we write. Notebook scribbling is private writing, but many people fear the consequences of being exposed should a husband, daughter, or mother violate this privacy. The result is stilted, wary, buttoned-up writing.

But there's another reason. When we write something, the words take on their own life. Stare back at us. Become real. Once we have written about a painful incident or disturbing realization it becomes much harder to make it vanish.

Rereading your notebook do you encounter only the most obvious, sanitized truths about your life? Are too many pages of your notebook poisoned by corporate-speak? Do your sentences sound exhausted from the effort you have had to expend to sound cheerful? Is there another, invisible notebook, more personal and dangerous, lurking beneath the surface of your words?

Dig deeper. You can use your notebook to explore the dark memories. Compromising situations. Aspects of yourself you'd prefer to forget. Troubling insights and revelations.

I am on a personal mission to write the truth in my notebook, even if it's an ugly truth:

Disturbing dream about D. and his alcoholism. In the dream D. was in labor, like a pregnant woman, and I was by his side, whispering encouragement. After a strenuous effort and much pain he finally delivered it—his liver.

In J. Kaplan's biography of Mark Twain he mentions a character who is "boyish and fundamentally conventional." Does that define me?

Brought the baby into the bank. I thought he looked adorable, all bundled up in his winter gear, but two women rolled their eyes and snickered at each other: "Look, he put the kid's hat on backwards." Made me feel male and small, in that order.

I visited Indonesia just after I had gotten married for the first time. At a dance recital in Bali I saw a young woman of astonishing beauty. In my notebook I wrote a long description of this woman and the mesmerizing effect she had on me. The entry ends with this sentence: "My *wedding ring burns like a neon coil.*"

Often we are tempted to write on a dangerous topic but the urge gets thwarted by a small inside voice that insists, *Oh no, I can't write about that.* Pay attention to this voice: it may be a sign that you're onto something.

I have been inspired to write about dangerous subjects by

Sharon Olds's poetry book *The Father*, a compassionate, unflinching frame-by-frame portrayal of her father's death. After reading this book I began a section in my notebook called Uncomfortable Prayers, for any idea that strikes me as out-of-bounds or taboo. Shortly thereafter I wrote this passage:

> Money has its own smell, all right, and the smell got pungent when I entered M., a "gated community." Five-acre zoning. No street signs. Private police force invisibly patrolling streets lined mansion after tremendous mansion, one bigger than the next. Towns like this one are America's dirty secrets, our white-only ghettos.

Don Murray has argued that one of the most important tools a writer can have is "disloyalty"—writing not what the subject would want us to say but what we honestly perceive about that subject. Writing difficult truths about people we love, even in a private notebook, can make us feel guilty and mean-spirited. At times I wonder if I haven't gone beyond disloyalty to outright betrayal as in a poem like this.

Splitting Wood
My younger brother taught me this:
Strike hard and always with the grain.
This works. The wood yields to the maul
like a kid's cartoon of wood splitting,
the pieces jumping apart
as if merely glued together.

I stack some kindling and catch
a splinter at the base of my hand,
my soft hands so unlike his.
I can picture him talking at me:
"Your poetry has no suffering in it."

His hard body has aged beyond mine
like a chunk of rough dry firewood
that consumes itself, burning too fast,

too fast to find a lover or wife,
too fast to have children
but only to delight in mine,
too fast to listen to anyone else
but only to talk talk talk
spilling out a head full of theories
nobody wants to hear, like a light left on
burning at noon in an empty room.

My brother lives alone in a small room
without a tv or telephone.

I start a fire the way he taught me:
shavings, the kindling cross-stacked,
no bark, never any paper.

On the stove's clean blue flame
I sterilize the blade of a small knife
and lean forward to dig out the splinter
which has rooted deeper than I thought.
I gasp at the blood, the pain. I cry.
My trembling hands struggle to cut out
that which is not, and is, part of me.

Sure it's hard to write from the honest part of your heart. But if you can't tell the truth in your notebook—at least some of the time—where can you tell it? And if your notebook doesn't reflect the marrow of your inner life, what good is it?

Final Thoughts

Kierkegaard tells how a head of lettuce, to have that succulent heart, requires time, leisure. He compares this to the meditation time, the dwelling in the inner life, that real human living requires.

William Stafford

Hippocrates once said that as human beings we are "obligate acrobes." When the body's supply of oxygen gets interrupted, even for a short time, our very lives are imperiled. We must breathe in order to survive.

In this spirit of survival, I have tried to suggest various ways a notebook can help a writer breathe in and out. But writer's notebooks aren't for everybody. Many writers find keeping a notebook as natural and essential as inhaling and exhaling; others find it tedious, confining, or distracting.

"This may not be the kind of quote you want for your book," one novelist told me, "but the way I see it you either write to get published or you write in your notebook. I can't see how you can do both. I sure can't."

This point is conceded: certainly a writer can survive without a writer's notebook. But you can't survive without an inner life. And keeping a notebook is one way to nurture that inner life. It's a place of ballast. Taproots. The nine tenths of your iceberg that never gets seen. The hidden aquifer that feeds your words.

There I go again: aquifer, iceberg, taproots, ballast. In this book I have put forth a smorgasbord of metaphors for a writer's notebook. There is something reminiscent of the Emperor's clothes about all this. I keep reminding myself: *It's no more than a book with a bunch of blank pages to write on.* At some point there's a risk of talking all the mystery out of the idea. The point of a writer's notebook is nothing more nor less than writing—first person and intimate, sincere or experimental—on a regular basis.

In Wallace Stegner's novel *Crossing to Safety* the narrator says to his wife: "If I'm going to set the literary world on fire, the only way to do it is to rub one word against another."

A writer's notebook is one place to start rubbing.

Bibliography

References on Writer's Notebooks

Asher, Sandy. *Where Do You Get Your Ideas?* New York: Walker, 1987.

Bender, Sheila. *The Writer's Journal.* New York: Bantam.

Boland, Eavan. "25 Circumstances for Survival," *Poets & Writers Magazine*, September/October 1995.

Chandler, Raymond. *The Notebooks of Raymond Chandler*, ed. Frank McShane. New York: Echo Press, 1976.

Cheever, John. *The Journals of John Cheever.* New York: Knopf, 1990.

Didion, Joan. *Slouching Towards Bethlehem.* New York: Farrar, Straus, 1961.

Dillard, Annie. *The Writing Life.* New York: Harper & Row, 1989.

Fitzgerald, F. Scott. *The Notebooks of F. Scott Fitzgerald*, ed. Matthew J. Bruccoli. New York: Harcourt Brace Jovanovich, 1978.

Fletcher, Ralph. *A Writer's Notebook: Unlocking the Writer Within You.* New York: Avon, 1996.

Gordon, Mary. "The Country Husband" [essay], *New York Times Book Review*, October 6, 1991.

Hemley, Robin. *Turning Life into Fiction.* Cincinnati: Story Press, 1994.

Holzer, B. N. *A Walk Between Heaven and Earth: A Personal Journal on Writing and the Creative Process.* New York: Bell Tower, 1994.

Junker, Howard, ed. *The Writer's Notebook*. San Francisco: ZYZZYVA, 1995.

Kafka, Franz. *The Diaries 1910–1923*, ed. Max Brod. New York: Schocken Books, 1948.

Kuusisto, Stephen, Deborah Tall, and David Weiss, eds. *Taking Note: From Poet's Notebooks*. A Special Issue of *Seneca Review*. Geneva, New York: Hobart and William Smith Colleges Press, 1991.

Mallon, Thomas. *A Book of One's Own: People and Their Diaries*. New York: Ticknor & Fields, 1984.

Oliver, Mary. *Blue Pastures*. New York: Harcourt Brace Jovanovich, 1995.

Plath, Sylvia. *The Journals of Sylvia Plath*, ed. Ted Hughes and Frances McCullough. New York: The Dial Press, 1982.

Rich, Adrienne. *What Is Found There: Notebooks on Poetry and Politics*. New York: W. W. Norton, 1993.

Sarton, May. *Journal of a Solitude*. New York: W. W. Norton, 1973.

Weil, Simone. *First and Last Notebooks*. London: Oxford University Press, 1970.

Woolf, Virginia. *A Writer's Diary by Virginia Woolf*, ed. Leonard Woolf. New York: Harcourt Brace Jovanovich, 1954.

Other Works Cited

Agee, James. *A Death in the Family*. New York: Putnam, 1956.

Allison, Dorothy. In *The Writer's Notebook*, ed. H. Junker. San Francisco: ZYZZYVA, 1995.

Baca, James S. *Working in the Dark: Reflections of a Poet of the Barrio*. Santa Fe: Red Crane Books, 1992.

Bly, Robert. Introduction to *The Darkness Around Us Is Deep: Selected Poems of William Stafford*, ed. Robert Bly. New York: HarperCollins, 1993.

Carver, Raymond. "Cathedral." In *Where I'm Calling From*. New York: Random House, 1986.

Dunn, Stephen. In *Taking Note: From Poet's Notebooks*, ed. Stephen Kuusisto, Deborah Tall, and David Weiss. A Special Issue of *Seneca Review*. Geneva, New York: Hobart and William Smith Colleges Press, 1991.

Fletcher, Ralph. *What A Writer Needs*. Portsmouth, NH: Heinemann, 1993.

———. *I Am Wings: Poems About Love*. New York: Atheneum, 1994.

———. *Fig Pudding*. New York: Clarion Books, 1995.

———. *Ordinary Things: Poems from a Walk in Early Spring*. New York: Atheneum, 1997.

———. *Spider Boy*. New York: Clarion Books, 1997.

———. *Twilight Comes Twice*. New York: Clarion Books, 1998.

Gardinier, Suzanne, 1994. *The Seventh Generation*. First printed in *The Kenyon Review*—New Series, Winter 1995, Vol. XVII, No. 1. Reprinted by permission of the author.

Hanh, Thich Nhat. *The Miracle of Mindfulness*. New York: Bantam, 1992.

Irving, John. *The World According to Garp*. New York: Ballantine Books, 1978.

Kaysen, Susanna. *Girl, Interrupted*. New York: Random House, 1993.

Kennedy, X. J. From *Taking Note: From Poet's Notebooks*, ed. Stephen Kuusisto, Deborah Tall, and David Weiss. A Special Issue of *Seneca Review*. Geneva, New York: Hobart and William Smith Colleges Press, 1991.

Lamott, Anne. *Bird by Bird*. New York: Random House, 1994.

McCarthy, Cormac. *The Crossing*. New York: Random House, 1994.

Morgan, Robert. From *Taking Note: From Poet's Notebooks*, ed. Stephen Kuusisto, Deborah Tall, and David Weiss. A Special

Issue of *Seneca Review*. Geneva, New York: Hobart and William Smith Colleges Press, 1991.

O'Brien, Tim. *The Things They Carried: A Work of Fiction*. Boston: Houghton Mifflin, 1990.

Olaleye, Isaac. *Bitter Bananas*. Honesdale, PA: Boyd Mills Press, 1994.

Olds, Sharon. Interview by Laurel Blossom. *Poets & Writers Magazine*, September/October 1993.

Rogers, Carl. *Freedom to Learn*. New York: Macmillan, 1983.

Rutsala, Vern. From *Taking Note: From Poet's Notebooks*, ed. Stephen Kuusisto, Deborah Tall, and David Weiss. A Special Issue of *Seneca Review*. Geneva, New York: Hobart and William Smith Colleges Press, 1991.

Stafford, William. *The Darkness Around Us Is Deep: Selected Poems of William Stafford*, ed. and intro. Robert Bly. New York: HarperCollins, 1993.

Stegner, Wallace. *Crossing to Safety*. New York: Random House, 1987.

Updike, John. *Brazil*. New York: Random House, 1994.

Wolff, Tobias. *The Pharoah's War*. New York: The Atlantic Monthly Press, 1989.